THE SHELBURNE
ESCAPE LINE

Radio Londres
BBC shortwave French language service
1900 hours, January 28, 1944:

"Bonjour tout le monde à la maison d'Alphonse"
("Good evening to everyone at the House of Alphonse.")

For two French-Canadian agents working with the French Resistance in Brittany, this apparently innocuous greeting was very welcome. It meant that MI-9 had given the go-ahead for the first of their long-planned pick-up operations. A Royal Navy Motor Gun Boat was steaming at full speed towards the Breton coast for a clandestine rendezvous later that night. Downed Allied aviators, hidden in local "safe houses," would be led under cover of darkness, to a secluded beach. The airmen didn't know it yet, but if all went well—if they got past the German patrols on the cliffs above, if no-one alerted the Gestapo—they would be back in England by the time the sun came up . . .

THE SHELBURNE ESCAPE LINE

SECRET RESCUES OF ALLIED AVIATORS BY THE FRENCH UNDERGROUND, THE BRITISH ROYAL NAVY & LONDON'S MI-9

RÉANNE HEMINGWAY-DOUGLASS
& DON DOUGLASS

Pen & Sword
AVIATION

First published in 2014 by Cave Art Press, Anacortes,
WA 98221, Washington, United States

Reprinted in this format in 2015 by
PEN & SWORD AVIATION
An imprint of
Pen & Sword Books Ltd
47 Church Street
Barnsley, South Yorkshire
S70 2AS

ISBN 978 1 47383 778 2

Typeset by Tony D. Locke, Armchair ePublishing, Anacortes, WA

Printed and bound in England
By CPI Group (UK) Ltd, Croydon, CR0 4YY

Pen & Sword Books Ltd incorporates the Imprints of Aviation, Atlas,
Family History, Fiction, Maritime, Military, Discovery, Politics, History,
Archaeology, Select, Wharncliffe Local History, Wharncliffe True Crime,
Military Classics, Wharncliffe Transport, Leo Cooper, The Praetorian Press,
Remember When, Seaforth Publishing and Frontline Publishing

For a complete list of Pen & Sword titles please contact
PEN & SWORD BOOKS LIMITED
47 Church Street, Barnsley, South Yorkshire, S70 2AS, England
E-mail: enquiries@pen-and-sword.co.uk
Website: www.pen-and-sword.co.uk

To the memory of Elwood (Woody) Blondfield

And to all those French people who risked
their lives in support of the Allied cause.

CONTENTS

LIST OF MAPS

ACKNOWLEDGMENTS

This book, which has been an ongoing and important project for the past seven years, would have become a lifetime hobby had it not been for the encouragement and the help of many friends and family. In particular, I must give my husband, Don Douglass, credit for his constant goading over the years, for his help in interviewing, and for his contributions to this book.

Merci beaucoup to all of my French friends in Brittany and Savoie, many of whom feature in this book. Thank you, also, to Pierre Montaz, who led me along the tortuous route taken by Resistance members who hid Ken Sorgenfrei and his crew from the Germans.

Thanks are due also to those who helped with my initial research: Geoff Warren of Comox B.C., who set me on the path to Canadian resources; Nancy Costello Scovill for providing me with photographs from her father's albums; and Beverly Patton Wand, who shared her father's personal papers and photos and provided me with a copy of Joseph (Job) Mainguy's handwritten account of the *Réseau Shelburne*.

I am grateful to the archivists, staff and volunteers at the many museums Don and I visited: in Canada, the Comox Air Force Museum; in France, the Mémorial de Caen, the Musée de la Résistance et de la Déportation in Picardie, the Musée de Dunkerque and the Musée de la Résistance Nationale in Champigny; in Britain, the Imperial War Museums in Duxford and London (special thanks to Stephen Walton and Ian Proctor, respectively).

To those friends and family who—as the manuscript finally began to see light—waded through first, second and then third versions of the manuscript, making cogent comments or correcting technical terms, I give a rousing thanks: Terry Browne, Bill Carlisle; Sean Collins, Bruce Evertz; Dian Fitzgerald; Sally Foster; Jean Gillingwators, Paul Giles; Mel Kowal; John Leone; Roderick Nash; Jill Princehouse; Sarah Stoner; Sarah van Praag; Earl Valentine; Katherine Wells, and Kathryn Wilkens. I am indebted to my brother, Thomas L. Hemingway, Brigadier General, USAF (Ret) for his part in researching MI-9 and the early Resistance

Lines, and to Major General John Altenburg US Army (Ret); Lt. Colonel John La Raia, USAF (Ret); and Brigadier General John Hurley, USAF (Ret) for their invaluable help in correcting military details, and for their other contributions to this book; and to Bebe Blondfield for answering last minute questions before we went to press, despite the sad passing of her beloved Woody.

And to the team, without whom this book would ever have seen the light, I can never say enough to thank you for "bailing" me out: my editor, Arlene Cook; Rae Kozloff, my research partner and proofer; Ken Morrison for his graphics and Tony and Karla Locke for their layout skills. *Un grand merci à Tous.* (A huge thank you to All.)

PART I

THE SHELBURNE ESCAPE LINE

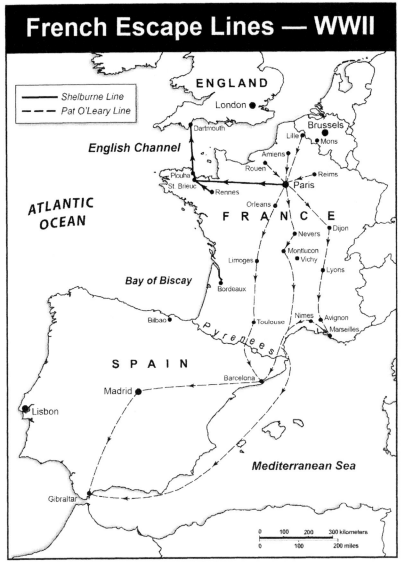

French Escape Lines — WWII

Legend:
—— Shelburne Line
- - - Pat O'Leary Line

ENGLAND
London
Dartmouth
English Channel
Brussels
Lille
Mons
Amiens
Rouen
Reims
Plouha
St. Brieuc
Rennes
Paris
ATLANTIC OCEAN
Orleans
FRANCE
Nevers
Dijon
Montlucon
Vichy
Lyons
Limoges
Bay of Biscay
Bordeaux
Nimes
Avignon
Toulouse
Marseilles
Bilbao
Pyrenees
SPAIN
Barcelona
Madrid
Lisbon
Mediterranean Sea
Gibraltar

0   100   200   300 kilometers
0   100   200 miles

Note: Escape Lines referred to in this book.

PROLOGUE

"Name? Rank? Serial number?" Questions flew rapidly and repeatedly at 23-year-old United States Army Air Force (USAAF) Pilot First Lieutenant Richard Smith. "Describe your squadron's insignia. What base did you come from in England? You told the driver who brought you here that your home is Minnesota. What's the name of your town? How far is it from Minneapolis? What's the name of the river in your town? What elementary school did you go to?"

Smith sat on a wooden stool in a small, darkened room on the second story of a Paris bistro. His interrogator paced back and forth, frowning at him. All Smith wanted to do was lie down and sleep. He had been in hiding for two weeks and he was tired, nervous and uncomfortable. The man questioning him spoke English without any trace of a French accent. He was short, with a black mustache and straight, slicked back hair. He had introduced himself as "Captain Hamilton," but he looked like pictures Smith had seen of Hitler. Who was he really, Smith wondered?

Smith's B-17 had been hit by anti-aircraft artillery in a bombing raid over Ludwigshafen, western Germany, in late December 1943. Smith managed to pilot the damaged plane across the border into northeastern France before giving the call to his crew: "Bail out! Bail out!" He lost sight of his men during the descent, but landed safely with three others in a field. French farmers hid them from the Germans for over a week and eventually turned them over to an Underground "agent." This man drove the four men to Paris and dropped them off at the house of an English-speaking woman, where a second agent—"Captain Hamilton"—was waiting to interrogate them.

Now, as Smith gave his answers to the man's relentless questions, he wondered whether he had really been delivered into the hands of the French Underground or if this was some kind of Gestapo plot. Hamilton knew where he lived in the States. He knew that a river ran through his town. Where did he get his information, and what the hell did it matter where Smith went to school?

The questions ended and Hamilton got up to leave. He told Smith to stay put. A few minutes later, a second man entered the room and fired off another round of questions, again in English, but this time with a heavy French accent. He stood so close that Smith could smell the garlic and cigarette smoke on his breath.

"Count using your fingers—show me the number one," the man demanded.

Smith raised his index finger.

"Now, show me the number three with your fingers."

Smith put his thumb and little finger together and held up his index, middle and ring fingers, the way Americans do.

The interrogator pulled a Gauloise out of a packet, lit it and offered it to him. Smith held the foul-smelling cigarette between his index and middle finger and coughed. "I'm sorry, Sir," he said. "I can't handle the odor."

Without knowing it, Smith had just passed two tests that proved he was American. He did not count with his fingers like a European, and he held the cigarette like a Yank.

The interrogator asked one more question, which Smith didn't understand. He began to sweat profusely, thinking he was done for. Finally, he told the man he didn't know the answer. His response, however, proved to be correct—he was not expected to know it.

Smith's nervousness was clearly visible. The interrogator stood up, assuring Smith that if he were an imposter, he would be killed at once. The man left the room without another word. Then a third interrogator entered. To Smith's surprise, she was an attractive young woman who introduced herself as "Claudette." In perfect English, with an American accent—Smith later learned that she had studied in the U.S. before the War—she began asking him yet more questions.

Smith answered them all without difficulty, after which "Claudette" told him he had answered all of their questions satisfactorily. He was obviously who he claimed to be—an American airman from Minnesota—and he and his fellow crewmen would eventually be sent back to their base in England. In the meantime, they would be photographed, given French clothing and shoes, false identification papers, and an Ausweis—a permit for the French coastal zone, in which travel was otherwise forbidden. They would have to wait in 'safe' houses until someone arranged transport for them. They might not all travel together.

Smith was relieved, but puzzled. He had no idea that his interrogators were agents of a highly secretive branch of the British Intelligence Service called MI-9, operating out of the British War Department in London. Nor did he know that Hamilton, the Hitler-like man who had fired the first round of questions at him, was a French Canadian, Lucien Dumais, or that he, Smith, would encounter this man yet again.

In fact, just a few days later, when Smith was huddled in the attic of a small stone cottage in Brittany with seventeen other downed Allied airmen, Dumais appeared, introducing himself to the group on this occasion as "Captain Harrison," and informing the airmen they would be leaving for England that very night, by boat from a nearby beach. There was no moon. They would have to drop down a cliff in the dark, being careful not to make a sound, as there were German patrols nearby.

Smith still had no idea who Hamilton/Harrison/Dumais really was, or that his imminent escape from Occupied France owed everything to this mysterious man and the small group of French people who worked with him.

Doubtless, the circumstances of their deliverance were discussed by all of the airmen aboard the Royal Navy motor gunboat that took them back to England. Only many years after the war would they learn that they were the first group to be evacuated by a new underground escape organization, of which Lucien Dumais was the leader. This was the "Shelburne Line," and it would prove to be one of the greatest secret success stories of World War II.

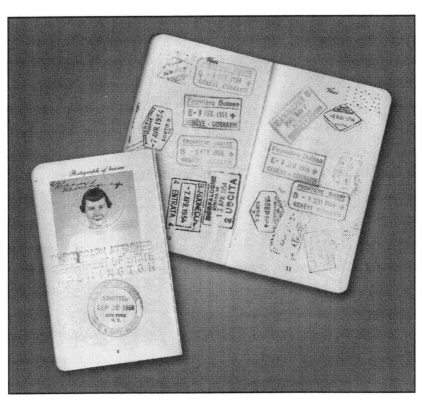

The author's passport, 1953

INTRODUCTION

In 1943, at the time Lieutenant Smith was shot down over France, and Lucien Dumais and his fellow Shelburne helpers were planning for their first evacuation operation, I was a child, safe in a two-story brick house in a suburb of Washington, D.C. I remember the War years as a time of rationing, blackouts, War Savings Bonds, test air raid drills, soldiers who lodged with us periodically, and neighbors who traded on the black market (to the disgust of my parents). Sometimes in the evening, I would sit with my parents listening to radio broadcasts from London by Edward R. Murrow, William L. Shirer and Eric Sevareid. Despite my young age, I was fascinated. Later I determined to learn as much as I could about what France and other countries had gone through during World War II.

Nine years after the war ended, I debarked in Cherbourg from the French ship, *Liberté*, to spend a year studying at the Université de Grenoble in the "capital of the Alps." After having cleared Customs in Paris and arranging for transport of my trunk to Grenoble, all with my then-meager command of French, I walked the streets of Paris.

Dim lights lined the boulevards and quays along the Seine River, and the streets were strangely quiet and devoid of pedestrians. Perhaps I walked right by the bistro where, a decade earlier, Lieutenant Smith had hidden in its icy attic.

Still recovering from World War II, the French lacked vehicles, fuel and money for luxury items and, when I returned to my bare-bones hotel that evening in Paris, I was shocked to find a box of cut newspaper squares in the toilet down the hall. (Soft toilet tissue came on rolls only in deluxe hotels.)

I had come to France to study French culture and history and to immerse myself in the life of the people. My home for twelve months would be a pension (a family-run boarding house) belonging to the Jouvent family in a hillside village named La Tronche, two miles above Grenoble. There, from my second-story balcony, I looked down upon the family's garden where potatoes, carrots, squash and tomatoes enhanced our nightly meals. Above Grenoble, I could sight the steep ramparts of the

Vercors that rise abruptly to the west and at night gaze upon the lights of the city that spread out in all directions from the banks of the Isère River.

Each day, after my classes at the university, I headed uphill to the Jouvent house on my three-speed vélo. I was eager to spend as much time as possible with my new "family"; playing their upright piano; teaching American songs to my 11-year-old "sister," Monique Jouvent; listening to recordings of operas and symphonies with Monsieur who would later become my "*Tonton*" (Uncle) Marcel.

But the highlights of these evenings were discussions about French politics and history; listening to accounts of the family's wartime experiences; hearing stories of the dreaded French Vichy Government Secret Police, the *Milice*, who were often as cruel to their own countrymen as the Nazi Gestapo. I learned of the terrible mass executions by the Nazis of Alpine Resistance members—their dead bodies hung from lampposts of along the quay of the Isère River which the Jouvents could see from their attic window. And I learned that for six long years the Jouvents never knew whom they could trust. I also heard accounts of French men and women who had risked not only their own lives but those of their families and friends to ensure that rescued Allied airmen would be returned safely to their bases and homelands in the fight to free France and Europe from Nazi occupation and oppression.

During that year, I became part of the Jouvent family—*la soeur américaine* (the American sister) and after twelve months of studying French, when I returned home to the States I knew I would always consider France my second country. In the decades that followed, I returned numerous times, either on my own or with my husband, Don, re-visiting my French family in Grenoble and sailing, bicycling and hiking throughout the country. On each visit I learned more about the war, recording in my journals the experiences of the Jouvents, their relatives and neighbors, and other friends. I was also introduced to still-living members of the French Resistance, as well as to Allied airmen whom they had rescued, and I wrote down their accounts as well. By the turn of the millennium, my journals were filled with stories, a few of which were known in France, but to my knowledge none had ever been printed in English.

One year, in the late 1980s, Don and I visited the summer cottage of my French "brother," Georges (Geo) Jouvent, and his wife Marie-Thérèse (Marité) Le Meur, in the town of Plouha, along the northeastern coast (Côte d'Armor) of Brittany. We had been there before, but on this occasion Geo and Marité told us the story of le Réseau Shelburne—the Shelburne Line. This was the code name for a wartime escape route from Paris to Plouha that saw 121 Allied airmen evacuated by sea from Nazi-occupied France within a period of eight months in 1944. It was this "line" that returned Lieutenant Smith to his base in England. A further 200 men escaped by overland routes, also with the assistance of Shelburne members. Shelburne is credited as the most successful of the World War II French escape lines for Allied aviators, in that it was never infiltrated by the Gestapo.

Don and I were both eager to know more. Plouha is a mere two miles from the coast, and Geo and Marité led us down the lane from their cottage to a path that was unmarked during the war but now bears the sign Sentier Shelburne (Shelburne Path). The Jouvents showed us the remnants—two crumbled stone walls—of the cottage known as la Maison d'Alphonse, a code name for the house where Allied aviators were hidden for a few hours before being led to nearby Anse Cochat (Cochat Cove) by local Resistance members. There, small wooden boats crewed by British sailors picked up the airmen from the beach, code-named Plage Bonaparte, and rowed them silently out to a Royal Navy vessel—Motor Gun Boat (MGB) 503—that waited offshore, ready to evacuate them to England.

These operations carried extreme risk. A German defense installation was perched on the cliff top at nearby Pointe de la Tour, northwest of Bonaparte Beach. Ammunition and gun fortifications still exist there. Though marked "off limits," the pillboxes continue to draw tourists—including Don and me—who ignore the safety warnings about the cliffs and crawl around on the mossy, dirty, graffiti-covered concrete.

I found the entire story fascinating, and Don and I made a point of walking the Chemin Shelburne whenever we returned to Plouha. However, we learned little more about the Shelburne Line itself on these visits—to me, it was like a jigsaw puzzle with many of the pieces missing. Then, in 2005, I came across a book titled, Par les Nuits les Plus Longues: Réseaux d'Evasions d'Aviateurs en Bretagne 1940-1944 (Through the

Shelburne Path

Pillbox, Pointe de la Tour

Longest Nights: Evasion Lines of Aviators in Brittany 1940-1944), by a French historian, Roger Huguen. The details contained within the book's 470 pages filled in many of the gaps in the Shelburne story, but still left mysteries to explore. They also led me to further accounts, some written by actual participants.

From Huguen's book I learned that, between 1940 and 1943, a series of Underground escape lines operated through Belgium, eastern France and the Atlantic Coast. They were known by code names such as Comet, Pat O'Leary (Pat Line), Oaktree (a branch of the Pat Line), and Burgundy. Some appeared, then vanished as tragic tortures and assassinations of members occurred; but as soon as one line was compromised, another sprang up.

Huguen introduced me also to the *convoyeurs* (guides) who led their *colis* ("packages" of Allied servicemen) along the escape lines out of Occupied Europe to safer territory; to the deprivations borne by French families who volunteered to hide, feed and clothe the men; to the utmost secrecy required to participate in any capacity; to Resistance members who endured torture or death if they were captured by the Nazi occupiers.

As I read the book in Plouha, in response to my comments and exclamations about what some of the people mentioned had personally experienced or endured during the war, Geo and Marité would reply, *"On les connaît"* ("We know them"), or *"C'est une cousine"* ("She's a cousin"), or *"C'était une camarade de classe"* ("She was a classmate"). More than once, they asked, "Do you want to meet this person?"

Of course! Don and I wanted to meet any of the participants who were still living. Thus began seven years of research and interviews that resulted in this book.

When I began this project in 2006, I found that records of names, places and locations were inconsistent or non-existent. Because combatants and intelligence agents were prohibited by secrecy laws from keeping written records until 25 years after the end of World War II, most of the early accounts were based strictly on memory. As a result, many discrepancies and errors exist in the accounts of the Shelburne and other escape lines, as written in the 1960s by members of the Resistance and MI-9, the British Intelligence Service's escape and evasion branch.

In later decades, British and American war records were unsealed, making it easier for both memoir writers and historians to verify facts. In 1974, the U.S. National Archives in Washington, D.C. declassified and released a swath of records to the American public—the so-called American Escape and Evasion Reports of U.S. airmen who had been evacuated to England through France or other European countries. And in 2010, the National Archives released digitized versions of most of these records, making them available on the Internet for the first time.

This veritable explosion of new information has resulted, in turn, in a flurry of new research into hitherto under-reported stories of World War II, including Resistance operations such as the Shelburne Line. Bookstore shelves now bend under the weight of new titles about World War II. In France, not only do these include books by French authors, but also translations of English-language authors. And still, new titles continue to appear.

So why produce another book on this period? Why did I, a non-historian, choose to write one? Because I felt the need to pass on the stories I have heard first-hand in France over the years, and to tell them through a Francophile lens. The stories in this book are of the men and women of the Shelburne Line who aided in the rescue of downed Allied airmen. Others are accounts of the aviators themselves. Still others are of ordinary French men and women—friends of mine—who were caught up in the war but survived to tell of their experiences. All are stories of quiet heroism and sacrifice that might otherwise be lost to history... stories, I believe, that deserve to be told.

Note: I have tried to follow as accurately as possible the details I gained in my research, both from written sources, as well as from interviews. In certain cases, I have taken the liberty of creating dialogue. I have also taken the liberty of using French spelling for towns and cities in France. Any mistakes are my own.—RHD

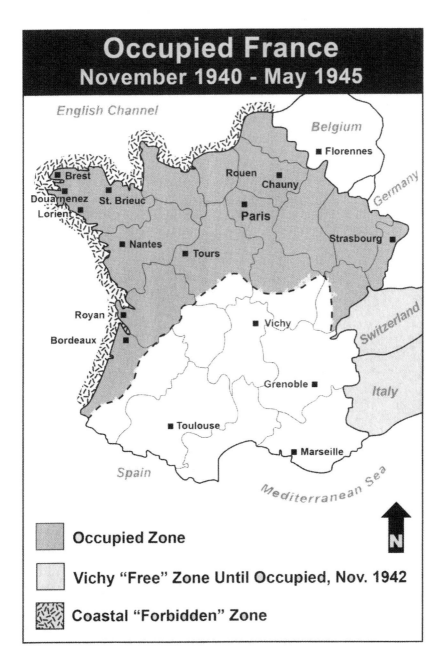

Occupied France
November 1940 - May 1945

English Channel

Belgium

Germany

Florennes

Rouen
Chauny

Brest

Douarnenez   St. Brieuc
Lorient

Paris

Nantes

Tours

Strasbourg

Royan

Vichy

Bordeaux

Switzerland

Grenoble

Italy

Toulouse

Marseille

Spain

Mediterranean Sea

N

Occupied Zone

Vichy "Free" Zone Until Occupied, Nov. 1942

Coastal "Forbidden" Zone

CHAPTER 1

MI-9 AND THE BRETON PLAN
FEBRUARY–SEPTEMBER 1943[1]

The Greatest Generation, a term coined by Tom Brokaw referring to the generation of Americans who fought the Second World War, has received a great deal of attention in print and in movies since the publication of his book of that name in 1998. Less attention, at least in the United States, has focused on the efforts of Europeans who, at great risk, helped Allied soldiers and airmen escape from Nazi-occupied Europe. These were not necessarily legendary figures of the Resistance who blew up trains and committed other acts of sabotage, but ordinary men and women who undertook the less glamorous but equally demanding and difficult tasks of hiding, feeding and transporting Allied personnel trying to find their way back to British soil. They were volunteers of all ages and from all walks of life, unable to take up arms in the war but determined to fight it in their own way. The risks were considerable. Captured helpers were routinely tortured by the Gestapo. Hundreds of them were arrested and executed or died in concentration camps. An unknown number died afterwards as a result of their imprisonment.

Nevertheless, by the end of the war more than 12,000 people from France, Belgium and the Netherlands had taken part in maintaining the various "escape and evasion" routes for Allied forces. Their contribution

---

1 This chapter was written with the assistance of my brother, Thomas L. Hemingway, Brigadier General, USAF, Ret., who did much of the research on MI-9 and the early escape lines.

to the Allied war effort was invaluable, particularly the return of pilots. More than 4,000 downed or captured Allied airmen and POWs ultimately escaped from Europe before the Allied D-Day landings in Normandy in June 1944, and an additional 3,000 escaped by 1945. The men themselves were grateful for their deliverance, while the regularity of their escapes represented an ongoing thorn in the side of Nazi Germany. None of this would have been possible without the men and women behind enemy lines who provided the necessary assistance, or the small number of intelligence agents in London and elsewhere who supported them in turn and transformed the escape lines from ad hoc local arrangements into organized, effective operations.

The need for escape lines, akin to the "underground railroads" of pre-Civil War America, first became necessary after thousands of British soldiers remained stranded in France after the evacuation from Dunkerque in May 1940. Many attempted to make their way to safer territory and headed for the unoccupied southeastern sector of France (administered until 1942 by the pro-Nazi government headquartered in Vichy), or to the neutral countries of Spain and Portugal. As the war intensified and Allied bombing raids commenced over Germany, escape lines were also needed to assist the return to Britain of downed air crews, particularly pilots, who were highly trained and desperately needed in the fight.

In France, the lines were operated by Resistance members and other volunteers, who provided "safe" houses, food, transport, and false identity papers, and funneled men from collecting points in Paris and other cities to the Spanish Pyrenees. Some lines sprang up spontaneously after Dunkerque, but by the middle of 1941, as the numbers of downed airmen in France continued to increase, and the lines posed both a drain on Resistance resources and a security risk to everyone involved, it was clear that some more formal oversight was required.

In Britain, a secret intelligence organization, MI-9 (shorthand for the British Directorate of Military Intelligence, Section 9), had been established early in the war, in December 1939, with the specific mission of aiding Allied servicemen stranded behind enemy lines. These could be either "escapees"—men who had spent at least some time in the hands of the Germans or their allies—or "evaders," who managed to avoid capture altogether. MI-9's initial tasks included the collecting of intelligence on Allied POWs; briefing personnel from all three branches of the British services on how to avoid capture; and developing "escape packs" to aid downed air crews. These packs typically included silk maps of various parts of Europe, cards printed with common phrases translated into assorted European languages, tiny compasses, water purification tablets, sewing supplies, Benzedrine tablets to combat fatigue, candy for energy, soap and a razor.

In the summer of 1941, MI-9's responsibilities expanded to include the organization and management of escape lines. A highly secret sub-branch was set up for this purpose and was referred to as "Room 900," after its official address (c/o Room 900, War Office)—in actuality, a cramped former tearoom within the British War Office building in Whitehall. Room 900's primary responsibilities were to set up new escape lines in northwestern Europe and to provide operational support for existing lines. In practice, this meant supplying Resistance personnel and other operatives with money, radio communications, and other supplies, and arranging "pick ups" of evaders and escapees, where feasible, from some locations behind enemy lines.

As the "nerve center" of escape line operations, Room 900 was staffed by two men, James Langley and Airey Neave. Both were British army officers who had escaped from the Germans after Dunkerque. Langley had lost an arm but made his way to Marseille, from where he was given passage to Spain by sympathetic Vichy officials. Neave was imprisoned for several months in the supposedly escape-proof fortress of Colditz, near Leipzig, but he too found a way to elude his captors and made his way to Switzerland.

Neave eventually returned to England via an extensive overland escape route known as the Patrick O'Leary (or Pat) Line, which had been established after Dunkerque and operated between Marseille and the Spanish Pyrenees. Some five hundred Allied servicemen ultimately made their way to Spain and Portugal along the Pat Line, but it required the participation of several hundred French volunteers, and it was constantly at risk of infiltration by German and Vichy agents. Room 900 provided funds to keep it and other escape lines in operation, but by mid-

CHAPTER 1

1942 the Pat Line collapsed altogether after a number of its operatives were betrayed by a British turncoat, Harold Cole.

By that time, the United States had joined the war in Europe and Allied bombing raids over Germany continued to intensify. This meant, in turn, that ever more air crews were being shot down, filling beyond capacity the "safe" houses operated by the French Resistance in Paris and elsewhere. The need to relieve the French of these men extended beyond the humanitarian imperatives for rescuing them. Air crews required extensive, lengthy and expensive training, and they were needed for the ongoing Allied war effort. Somehow they had to be brought back to British soil.

In southern France, in the autumn of 1942, surviving members of the Pat Line participated in two successful maritime "pick up" operations, in which a hundred men were retrieved from the coast near Marseille by the Royal Navy. In the months that followed, as the Germans occupied the remainder of France, Langley and Neave, in Room 900, began to envision similar, even more daring operations from the coast of Brittany directly across the English Channel, that would reduce the time required to repatriate the airmen as compared to the long routes to Spain and Gibraltar. Such operations would require a land component—an escape line from Paris to the pick-up location in Brittany—and the use of small, fast Royal Navy Motor Gun Boats. Langley set to work planning the logistics and by the late summer of 1943, with the number of downed airmen in France continuing to increase, he and Neave were ready to put their Breton plan into effect.

Room 900 gave its first plan for sea evacuations from Brittany the code name "Oaktree." As an escape line it was ultimately a failure, but Oaktree provided the basis for a succeeding line—Shelburne—that proved to be far more effective.

The operational heart of Oaktree was to be the Côte d'Armor, on the northeast coast of Brittany. The specific focus was the Baie de Saint-Brieuc (Bay of St. Brieuc), between the cities of St. Brieuc and Paimpol. There were several reasons for this choice. One was that the Royal Navy had identified several potential locations in the bay for discreet night-time "pick ups."

Another was that this stretch of coast was the center of an active local Resistance group that had been hiding airmen since 1941. Before the Pat O'Leary Line collapsed entirely, one of its operatives in northern France had made contact with the group's leader, François Le Cornec, and Room 900 was hopeful that Le Cornec might be agreeable to running the Breton end of a new escape line.

Langley assigned responsibility for contacting Le Cornec, for setting up the collection end of Operation Oaktree in Paris, and for assessing the Baie de Saint-Brieuc beaches *in situ*, to a man named Vladimir Bouryschkine.

Bouryschkine was of Russian origin but had grown up in the United States and become an American citizen. He was strongly built, charming and extremely garrulous. At the outbreak of the war he had been in Europe working for the American Red Cross as a physical education instructor. Opting to remain in Unoccupied France as a basketball coach to political prisoners, he eventually became a guide on a section of the Pat O'Leary Line in southern France.

After the Pat Line's collapse, Bouryschkine made his way to England. He had a reputation for being impetuous, but Airey Neave thought that, given training, he had "considerable possibilities" as an agent for Room 900. Langley agreed, and gave him the *nom de guerre* Val Williams, after the author of a series of popular 1930s adventure stories.

As Williams, Bouryschkine was briefed on how to organize links between Resistance personnel in Paris and Brittany. He was also given parachute and night-landing training. Landing successfully in France would only be the beginning of the operation, however. Thereafter, he would be required to design an evacuation route using rail transport between Paris and Brittany, with Resistance helpers serving as guides and operating safe houses at both ends. A number of safe houses were already in existence in Paris, but with the collapse of the Pat Line and the uncertain security of other lines, Room 900 decided that new ones would need to be found for the Oaktree Line. Williams would also have to provide money and supplies to the safe houses, and to train evaders to act and look like Frenchmen—all within a country crawling with Gestapo agents. It was not a job for the faint-of-heart, or, as it turned out, for someone of Williams' impulsive character. Williams was later

5

described by his successor in France, Lucien Dumais, as lacking all notion of good sense and having ignored the rules he had learned from MI-9, once he crossed the Channel back into France.

Langley paired Williams with a tall, square-jawed, radio ("wireless") operator, Raymond Labrosse. Twenty-two years old, Labrosse was an even-tempered French-Canadian signals sergeant recruited from Canadian Military Headquarters in London. He too had worked on the Pat O'Leary Line and was to become a valuable agent for Room 900. Good radio operators were in short supply within the British intelligence services, and Labrosse, who spoke French, proved to be cool-headed under pressure and a good partner for the more excitable Williams.

In the early spring of 1943, Williams and Labrosse made nine failed attempts to parachute into France from RAF Halifax aircraft. On every occasion, the pilot was unable to locate the landing zone due to fog and haze. Finally, at the end of February 1943, the two men landed successfully near Rambouillet, southwest of Paris. They were carrying money, false identity cards, revolvers and large quantities of cigarettes, to be used in the recruitment of local helpers. Two bicycles were dropped with them, although one was destroyed when its parachute failed to open.

Williams took the usable bicycle and cycled off to Paris, leaving Labrosse behind. Their plan was for Williams to establish a collection point for Allied airmen in Paris from which they could be transported by train to Brittany, while Labrosse established radio contact with London. However, the radio set Labrosse brought with him was damaged on landing and out of commission. Room 900 was unaware Williams and Labrosse had landed safely until they received a message from Williams, via the French Underground, in which he requested a new radio set for Labrosse. In the meantime, Williams made contact with Paul Campinchi (code named "François"), a Paris lawyer and Resistance leader, who agreed to oversee the collection of airmen for transport to Brittany.

While Room 900 considered the problem of getting a new radio to Labrosse, Williams and Campinchi traveled to Brittany, where they learned that a group of 39 British and American airmen was hidden in an 18th century chateau near Paimpol, with another 50 or so lodged in the vicinity. The chateau was the home of Countess Betty de Mauduit, a

Scottish-born American (née Roberta Laurie) married to a Frenchman, Count Henri de Mauduit, who had escaped to England in 1940 to serve with the Free French under General Charles de Gaulle. Williams proposed evacuating these men by sea from the Baie de Saint-Brieuc area, but his cavalier "borrowing" of radios belonging to other groups was deemed a security risk and he was otherwise unable to contact London.

In the meantime, the threat of infiltration increased by the day as, unbeknownst to Williams, the surviving Breton branch of the collapsed Pat O'Leary Line was compromised. The traitor—a German agent, Roger Le Neveu, known as "Roger Le Légionnaire"—was responsible for the arrests of a number of Breton Resistance members in the spring and summer of 1943. Those betrayed by Le Neveu included Betty de Mauduit, who was arrested by the Gestapo in June 1943 and sent to the Ravensbruck concentration camp, though she ultimately survived the war.

Unable for the time being to evacuate any of the airmen from the chateau by sea, Williams decided, out of desperation, to move some of them by train to the south of France from where they could continue on to Spain and Gibraltar via one of the still-operating overland lines. Williams recruited local guides and set off with four men himself—two Americans and two Poles—but he was arrested en route on June 4, allegedly as a result of his carelessness.

Imprisoned by the Gestapo and brutally interrogated, he maintained the cover story that he was an RAF officer who had been shot down over France and had joined the Resistance.

In Brittany, prior to his capture, Williams had made contact with Georges (Geo) Jouanjean, a Resistance member who agreed to work on the Oaktree escape line. Because of Williams' arrest, Oaktree was never implemented as a sea evacuation operation. However, Jouanjean and others worked on the land component of the Oaktree Line and ultimately helped to evacuate more than 60 Allied aviators—including Gordon Carter, an English-Canadian RAF officer, who would eventually become Jouanjean's brother-in-law, and whose story is told in Chapter 9 of this book. Like many of his colleagues, Jouanjean, too, was eventually betrayed by Roger Le Légionnaire and arrested and tortured by the Gestapo. Captured in June 1943, he spent a year in various French prisons before being transported to Auschwitz. This was merely the first of three German concentration camps to which he was sent. Jouanjean was later transferred to Buchenwald, then to Flossenburg, where more than 1,900,000 people in total died of torture, gassing, poison or experimental medical "treatments." Fortunately, Jouanjean was among the survivors when Flossenburg was liberated in May 1945.

With Williams' capture, the Oaktree plan collapsed even before its inception. Raymond Labrosse was still in Brittany, but in July 1943, having narrowly escaped being arrested with Geo Jouanjean, he headed for Spain. Against MI-9's instructions, he took with him a group of 27 airmen, successfully shepherding them across the Pyrenees and on to Gibraltar, from where they managed to return to England in September 1943.

Oaktree was not a complete failure, even so. Although no sea evacuations had been carried out, and Roger Le Légionnaire had decimated several of the Breton Resistance groups, many of the airmen hiding in Brittany made it to Spain, and the Paris and Breton ends of the Oaktree Line remained intact, under Paul Campinchi and François Le Cornec, respectively. Labrosse persuaded Langley and Neave that the plan for sea evacuations should proceed, and he volunteered to return to Brittany as the radio operator. The new operation, incorporating both the escape line from Paris to Brittany and the sea component across the southwestern end of the English Channel, was assigned the code name "Shelburne," after an 18th century British Prime Minister. Shelburne also happened to be the name of a town in Canada, which Airey Neave thought was appropriate given that his two principal operatives— Labrosse and a new recruit, Lucien Dumais—were from that country.

Neave himself had assumed the position of Room 900's senior officer by that time, as James Langley was transferred in September 1943 to work in another branch of MI-9. Neave's new partner in the War Office tearoom was Patrick Windham-Wright, a British army captain who had been awarded the Military Cross for his part in the Libyan campaign of 1942. Like Langley, Windham-Wright had lost an arm but this did not preclude his becoming an active agent in Shelburne evacuation operations.

Raymond Labrosse's new boss in France was to be Sergeant-Major Lucien Dumais, who would assume Williams' role as organizer of the Shelburne Line. Like Labrosse, Dumais was a French-Canadian and a member of the elite Fusiliers Mont-Royal. No stranger to Europe, he had participated in the ill-fated Allied raid on the occupied French port of Dieppe in August 1942. The raid was intended to serve as a precursor to a larger invasion but was poorly conceived and executed. Of the 6,000 Allied troops who participated, most of them Canadians, over 2,000 were captured by the Germans and more than 1,000 were killed.

Dumais was one of those captured by the Germans, but he escaped by jumping off the train transporting him to a POW camp in Germany. Scavenging off the land, he made his way to Marseille and eventually back to England. After being interrogated by MI-9, Langley offered him the task of working with the French Resistance. Dumais declined the offer and served instead as an observer with his old Canadian Army unit in North Africa. He disliked his new commanding officer, however, to the extent that upon his return to England in the summer of 1943, he re-established contact with MI-9. As Dumais was later to write, "there are more ways of fighting an enemy than shooting him."

At just 5 feet 2 inches (1.57 meters), Dumais was the minimum height for military service, but his stature had given him the ability to fight for himself since childhood, and he was quick to establish his authority. At 38—older than the airmen with whom he would come into contact—his age would also make him a less noticeable target for the Germans than young Frenchmen who, if caught, were subject to deportation to work camps. France, by that time, was the largest supplier of foreign male labor in Germany, and it was crucial to the success of the operation that Dumais not attract attention. It was of further help that his French-Canadian accent resembled the French spoken in Brittany.

Dumais liked Ray Labrosse immediately and admired the young man's courage and strength of character. The fact that Labrosse had brought the 27 airmen with him out of France, rather than setting forth for Spain on his own after the collapse of the Oaktree operation, suggested to Dumais that he would be dependable in a crisis. Labrosse, similarly, saw Dumais as someone he could work with.

The two men underwent weeks of intensive training for their new mission. This included parachuting from low altitude; firearm drills; exercises in following, evading, disarming suspects; burglarizing and safe-cracking in the dark; and, above all, constant practice in coding, decoding and interrogation. Dumais asked Room 900 to give them each their own personal code and key for contacting London in case they became separated. He also insisted that Labrosse test the radio equipment before they left England. Past directives from MI-9 had not included either, despite the fact that the radio tubes and filaments of the time were notorious for their lack of reliability, as Labrosse knew well from the Oaktree operation.

Labrosse was sent to Scotland to try out his equipment and skill at coding and decoding. The test proved critical, as the radio failed and Labrosse had to return to London for a replacement, delaying the departure date for France.

Dumais, in the meantime, was subjected to a test of a different sort. After spending a twenty-four hour period of leave in Surrey, he met with Windham-Wright back in London. As Dumais himself told the story, Windham-Wright hammered into him:

"Where were you yesterday? I phoned your room and there was no reply."

Silence.

"Were you seeing a girl?"

Dumais nodded.

"Her name and address?"

Dumais thought this was going too far and told Windham-Wright it was "a personal matter."

Windham-Wright was unsympathetic. "With us," he said, "there is no such thing."

Dumais was subsequently advised that women were trouble and there was only one safe rule—"Have nothing to do with them." He was also told that if he couldn't abide by this rule, "don't tell them about your work." Dumais recalled that "not being a monk or a eunuch, I took due note."

Other elements of his MI-9 training included being approached by strangers in pubs, who bought him drinks and then tried to pump him for information. He was arrested by the police on made-up charges and left to stew in a cell. He was accused of carrying false military papers and was provoked in other ways. All were tests of his reactions and responses under pressure.

At the conclusion of these exercises, Windham-Wright offered Dumais an exit. Dumais was old enough to retire from active service. He could serve as a training officer in his old unit. It would be the most sensible thing.

Was this some further test? Dumais wasn't sure, but he had no intention of quitting, and said so.

Windham-Wright was satisfied. "Fine," he replied. "Glad to have you with us."

Dumais was "in." The Shelburne operation could begin.

A TOUS LES FRANÇAIS

La France a perdu une bataille!
Mais la France n'a pas perdu la guerre!

Des gouvernants de rencontre ont pu capituler, cédant à la panique, oubliant l'honneur, livrant le pays à la servitude. Cependant, rien n'est perdu!

Rien n'est perdu, parce que cette guerre est une guerre mondiale. Dans l'univers libre, des forces immenses n'ont pas encore donné. Un jour, ces forces écraseront l'ennemi. Il faut que la France, ce jour-là, soit présente à la victoire. Alors, elle retrouvera sa liberté et sa grandeur. Tel est mon but, mon seul but!

Voilà pourquoi je convie tous les Français, où qu'ils se trouvent, à s'unir à moi dans l'action, dans le sacrifice et dans l'espérance.

Notre patrie est en péril de mort.
Luttons tous pour la sauver!

VIVE LA FRANCE !

JUIN 1940
LONDRES

GENERAL DE GAULLE

General De Gaulle's "call" to the French, broadcast from London on June 18, 1940, translates loosely as follows: The government has capitulated, giving in to panic, forgetting honor, delivering the country to servitude. However, nothing is lost, because this war is a world war. In the free universe, immense forces have yet to give in. One day they will crush the enemy. France must be present on that victorious day. Then, she will regain her liberty and her grandeur. That is my goal, my only goal! That is why I ask all French people, no matter where they may be, to join me in action, in sacrifice and in hope. Our country is in deathly peril. Let us all fight to save her! VIVE LA FRANCE!

The Vichy government minted new coins, replacing the words Liberty, Equality, Fraternity on the French Franc with Work, Family, Fatherland. The French Republic was also renamed the French State.

CHAPTER 2

SETTING UP THE SHELBURNE LINE
NOVEMBER 1943–JANUARY 1944

At midnight on November 19, 1943, two RAF Lysander aircraft departed London for a drop at a small, clandestine, dirt landing strip 60 miles northeast of Paris. Aboard the lead airplane were Lucien Dumais and Raymond Labrosse. Their drop mission was code-named "Magdalen II." Two previous attempts to land them in France had failed due to fog and muddy conditions. Now, cramped in the stern of the lead Lysander, with their baggage at their feet, the two men doubled up like monkeys in a tree, prepared for an uncomfortable crossing of the English Channel.

RAF Lysander over France, WWII. Lysanders were the workhorses of covert nighttime operations.

Lysanders were small, high-winged, single-engine aircraft with room for a pilot and a single passenger. One or two additional passengers could be carried, but they had to squeeze into the tail end of the fuselage where conditions were extremely cramped. The Lysanders flew at a maximum speed of just over 200 mph (320 kmh), meaning that by day they were easily picked off by the much faster German Messerschmitt fighters. By night, however, Lysanders were regularly used for parachute drops and pick-up and contact missions in France, where they would land in fields or other short strips of land marked out by handheld flashlights. The Lysander pilots navigated by compass and dead reckoning, so missions into France were carried out on moonlit nights when there was some visibility. The aircraft were initially painted black, in the mistaken belief that this would render them invisible at night. However, Dumais' and Labrosse's pilot, Hugh Verity, later wrote in his wartime memoir, *We Landed by Moonlight,* that "the black silhouette against low cloud was far too positive. So I had the upper surfaces re-camouflaged in dark green and pale grey." Attention to such detail proved that these pilots did not accept conventional wisdom, but thought for themselves.

The two Lysanders approached their destination a little over an hour after take-off. The landing field was a strip of dirt outside the town of Chauny, in the Oise Valley. The lead plane made one pass around, blinked its lights on and off once, and waited as a series of lights flashed from the ground, indicating the direction for touchdown. Both planes landed safely, then taxied to the end of the strip and stopped. The two passengers in the first Lysander uncoiled their legs and jumped out, Dumais clutching his briefcase, and Labrosse his radio. Both men were eager to begin their mission. Included in their pockets or baggage were their false IDs, demobilization papers, used Paris *Métro* (subway) tickets, two miniature compasses, road maps, tear-gas fountain pens, a wire metal saw (hidden in the seams of their trousers), and escape ropes made into the soles of espadrille-like slippers. Both men also carried money to pay for their expenses, as well as for food for the French agents and families who would hide the airmen.

Awaiting their arrival were four French ground crew. "Follow," they whispered, and reached for the two men's bags before heading toward the end of the runway.

"Leave that alone!" Labrosse growled, as one of the Frenchmen grabbed his radio case. This was a piece of equipment Labrosse would never let out of his sight, just as Dumais would always carry his own briefcase.

As Dumais and Labrosse were shown into a waiting truck, the two Lysanders took off for their return flight to London with six new passengers aboard: three USAAF airmen, two from the RAF, and a Belgian MI-9 agent, Captain Dominique Potier. Dumais was impressed with the efficiency of the operation, which had taken no more than five minutes and had been perfectly executed. Even then, no one needed reminding of the risks involved. In *We Landed by Moonlight*, pilot Hugh Verity followed up his account of the "Magdalen II" mission with the fact that Potier parachuted back into France a month later (December 1943), but was betrayed and arrested by the Germans. According to Verity, Potier was "terribly tortured" but refused to reveal information. "After they had gouged out one of his eyes, he killed himself by jumping from the second floor of Frèsnes prison." Suicide was often the only way Resistance members caught and tortured by the Nazis were able to keep from "talking." Dumais and Labrosse knew this as well as anybody.

From their landing site in Chauny, Dumais and Labrosse were taken by their driver to a safe house, where they would hide until local Resistance members gave them the go-ahead to travel to Paris. Their French hosts pumped them in the meantime for knowledge about the anticipated Allied invasion, how strong the Allies really were, and what was happening in England, though Dumais and Labrosse could tell them little.

They had also been drilled to leave their real identities behind in England and to think and act only as their new ones. "As I tried to assume my new personality and live with it," Dumais wrote later, "my contact with my old, true self began to grow weaker; . . . once I stepped out of England, I would cease to be Lucien Dumais…" His "official" French identity was that of Lucien Jules Desbiens, an undertaker. The identity card produced for him by MI-9 showed him sober and serious in a suit and tie, with slicked black hair parted on the left. He wore eyeglasses and had grown a mustache for the mission.

Labrosse was transformed into Marcel Desjardins, sales representative for a French medical equipment company.

To the Resistance agents they would meet in France, Dumais and Labrosse would be known only as "Léon" and "Claude," respectively, and at times they would invent other names to confuse the enemy, as well as any prospective infiltrators.

Setting up the Shelburne Line would be a two-part process. One was to organize the Paris end of the line. The other was to travel to the Breton town of Plouha to meet the local Resistance leader, François Le Cornec— who had been approached previously by Val Williams—and study a nearby beach as a potential pick-up location.

Paris came first, and after two days in Chauny, the two men received clearance to travel to the capital. They planned to meet there with Paul Campinchi, the lawyer and former head of the Paris Resistance who, like Le Cornec, had been contacted by Val Williams during the failed Oaktree operation. Fearing that Campinchi might have been compromised by Williams' arrest, Room 900 had told Dumais not to connect with him immediately. However, Labrosse, who had worked closely with Campinchi during his previous stint in France, trusted him implicitly and convinced Dumais that they should contact him as soon as possible.

Although happy to reconnect with Labrosse, Campinchi was wary of Dumais. The men met in a café where Dumais described the plans for the Paris end of the proposed Shelburne operation. After an evening of heated discussions, the two men were convinced of each other's integrity, and Dumais asked Campinchi if he would lead the Paris component of the evacuation line. However, the lawyer, who had been forced into hiding for six months with his family after Williams was caught, wanted time to think it over before he gave his answer.

Campinchi mentioned Williams' imprudent behavior, saying that the Oaktree chief had talked about his mission to anyone who wanted to listen. Seemingly the only blunder he had not made was to put ads in the newspaper to recruit MI-9 agents. In Campinchi's opinion, it had been just a matter of time before Williams got caught, forcing many other agents to go into hiding.

A few days later, Campinchi agreed to assume responsibility for the Paris end of the Shelburne Line. His tasks would consist of locating safe houses in which to lodge the evaders and training his operators to interrogate them. Dumais had studied the security weaknesses in other evacuation lines and was determined to prevent the same problems with Shelburne. All rescued aviators would be questioned as they passed through Paris. Those who passed their "test" would be outfitted with appropriate clothing and shoes, furnished with false ID cards and German *Ausweis* (permits to travel within restricted coastal zones), and generally taught to act like Frenchmen. Two guides (*convoyeurs*) would then accompany the "packages" (*colis*)—as the airmen were called—by train to St. Brieuc, at the southeast end of the Côte d'Armor. There a local agent would meet them and disperse them among safe houses in the vicinity. While on the train, the airmen would feign being deaf-mutes if someone spoke to them, or pretend to be asleep. Both were highly risky strategies, but no one could think of better ones.[1]

With the Paris end of Shelburne arranged, Dumais and Labrosse traveled the 250 miles (400 kilometers) to Plouha to meet with François Le Cornec. Two miles from the coast, Plouha was home to approximately 4,000 people. Le Cornec owned a café and butcher shop in the town and served as head of the local Resistance organization. Mobilized in 1939 at age 34, he had been captured by the Germans soon after the Occupation in 1940 and sent to a *Stalag* (POW camp) in Germany. As a prisoner, he managed to falsify his military papers to show that he had served in the Great War in 1918. Convincing his captors that he was too old to be held as a POW, he was sent back to Brittany to "serve" as a farmer. France provided much of Germany's food needs during the war, and Le Cornec would help produce French wheat and vegetables for German consumption.

Le Cornec's own preference, upon returning home to Plouha, was to join the Free French forces, headed by General Charles De Gaulle in London. However, his attempts to escape to England by boat were unsuccessful, so his desire to fight was transmuted into the organization of a Resistance group comprised of his friends in the region and two local Plouha *gendarmes*.

---

1 So many "deaf-mutes" rode the trains in France it was a miracle none of the German soldiers ever caught on.

Dumais and Labrosse explained their needs for the Breton component of Shelburne, and Le Cornec agreed to put together a local group to support the evacuation operations. His responsibilities were numerous. He would have to find and train guides to help in the evacuations, find safe houses in Plouha and the surrounding area in which to lodge the airmen, locate a means of transportation for those housed beyond the vicinity of the town, and find someone who could falsify and print documents when necessary.

Dumais explained that priority for evacuees would be as follows: pilots first, then navigators, other crew, and last, agents in danger, or others who were needed for additional training and/or jobs in England. Dumais also assured Le Cornec that MI-9 would provide money to help the host families pay for food—much of which could be obtained only at high prices on the black market—and that cases of ammunition and other supplies for local Resistance operations would be brought in by the British boats with each pick-up operation.

With these arrangements agreed upon, Le Cornec took Dumais to study the adjacent coastline. Fragmented and precipitous, the Plouha stretch follows a general east-west direction and includes some of Brittany's highest cliffs—some 60 meters (200 feet) or more. In spite of this, the Royal Navy had determined from maps and aerial photographs supplied by the RAF that a nearby cove, Anse Cochat, might be a suitable location for discreet nighttime pick-ups off the beach. Such operations would be undertaken by men rowing small wooden surfboats, dispatched from a larger Royal Navy Motor Gun Boat (MGB) waiting offshore.

Two of Le Cornec's colleagues in Plouha, Pierre Huet, a former French military pilot, and Joseph ("Job") Mainguy, a merchant navy captain, who were both familiar with Anse Cochat, convinced Dumais of its suitability for the evacuation operations. The shingled beach at the bottom—which would be given the code name "Bonaparte"—blended into a wide expanse of sand at low tide, acceptable for surfboats. There were also several caves in which men could be hidden while waiting for the boats. This was important, as the cliffs above were patrolled by the Germans, who had constructed a series of four concrete pillboxes on Pointe de la Tour, a rocky promontory that juts out above the sea a mile northwest of Anse Cochat. The pillboxes were manned by White Russian conscripts—anti-Stalinists, who sympathized more with Nazi ideals than with Soviet Communism—and their fortifications housed cannons, machine guns, ammunition bunkers, searchlights and living space.

A second and smaller German outpost lay about a mile southeast of Anse Cochat, but out of sight of Bonaparte Beach.

Halfway between Anse Cochat and Plouha, was a small stone cottage that could be used as a collection point for airmen hidden in the town and surrounding area prior to each "Bonaparte" evacuation operation. Code-named *la Maison d'Alphonse* (the House of Alphonse), the cottage was uninhabited but belonged to Jean Gicquel, a fisherman who was one of Le Cornec's trusted friends. Gicquel and his pregnant young wife Marie (Mimi) agreed to move into the cottage and provide a cover for the Shelburne group's activities. Both the relative seclusion of the *Maison d'Alphonse* and its proximity to the beach proved to be critical to the success of the subsequent evacuation operations.

The path (named *Chemin Shelburne* after the War) from the *Maison d'Alphonse* to Anse Cochat led through a six-foot-high "tunnel" of heather, nettles and Scotch broom that opened a half-mile later to a flatland of farmers' fields.[2] It then crossed an old Customs path to the edge of a perpendicular scree-slope. At the foot of this drop, slightly above the high tide line, was a long indentation and a cave where the evacuees would be able to hide just out of sight of the pillboxes on Pointe de la Tour.

Peering over the scree-slope with Le Cornec, Dumais voiced concern about the dangerous descent and the likely conditions of the path in rain or snow. Le Cornec replied that before each evacuation, local guides would instruct the airmen on how to make their descent. "If the guides can do it," he said, "I'm sure the rest of us can."

At low tide, a long gully (*goulet*) running laterally to Anse Cochat could serve as an alternate route for the returning guides whenever equipment sent from London was too heavy to carry up the scree-slope. At high tide, however, the entrance to the gully was impassable from the

---

2 The original Customs path leading from St. Brieuc to Paimpol is now part of the protected *Sentiers de Grande Randonnée*. It, too, is lined with weeds and prickly shrubs.

beach, but Le Cornec assured Dumais that, as with the scree-slope, they would manage somehow.

For Dumais and Labrosse, Le Cornec's assurances meant that the plans for the entire Shelburne Line were now in place. Leaving Le Cornec in charge in Plouha, the two French-Canadians returned to Paris, where they sent radio confirmation to London and awaited orders from MI-9 to carry out the first Bonaparte evacuation operation. It was now late November. Neave had told Dumais to prepare for the first evacuation in December, as large numbers of airmen were known to be in hiding in both Paris and Brittany, posing an ongoing danger to the people who housed them. MI-9—and Room 900—had also been apprised of the possibility of an Allied invasion the following spring. This meant it was essential to evacuate as many men as possible in the months ahead, though Neave did not inform Dumais of this specific reason.

Before Dumais and Labrosse left London, it had been agreed that when MI-9 was ready to schedule an evacuation, a message would be sent via the BBC radio program, *Les Français Parlent aux Français* ("The French Speak to the French"). Listening to the BBC was a punishable offense in France, but people with radios tuned in anyway to obtain news of the outside world beyond the propaganda issued by the Germans and the Vichy government. "The French Speak to the French" was broadcast nightly across the Channel at 7 p.m. and repeated at 9 p.m. Each broadcast included songs, poems and nonsensical phrases that were meaningful as coded messages to the various cells of Underground organizations across France.

For the Bonaparte operations, the message *Bonjour tout le monde à la maison d'Alphonse* (Good evening to everyone at the house of Alphonse) meant an evacuation operation was to take place that night. *Yvonne always thinks of the happy occasion* meant the evacuation was postponed for twenty-four hours. *Rigoulet has a good head* meant the operation, if scheduled, was canceled.

December arrived, but the weather was incessantly stormy. Night after night came the same message over the BBC, *Yvonne pense toujours à l'heureuse occasion.* In London, Paris and Plouha, everyone involved with the Shelburne Line was asking the same questions. Would the gales ever cease? How many airmen were now in hiding? Would the audacious evacuation plan even succeed?

Dumais and Labrosse were the only two people in France who knew the code phrase that would mean the green light for the Bonaparte operations. Every night they waited to hear *Bonjour tout le monde…*, but as December 1943 passed into January 1944, the storms continued and still the announcer on the BBC spoke only of *Yvonne*.

Anse Cochat at low tide.

The goulet (ravine) *was impassable at high tide.*

Brittany Region / *Forbidden Coastal Zone*

Paimpol

Le Bois de la Salle

St-Malo

Plouha

Guingamp   St-Brieuc

Brest

Limit of
Forbidden
Costal Zone

Douarnenez

Pontivy

Rennes

Quimper

Lorient

FRANCE

Area of
Detail

0   50 kilometers

0   50 miles

N

24

CHAPTER 3

THE GREEN LIGHT
OPÉRATION BONAPARTE I
JANUARY 28, 1944

As January 1944 arrived and the message on the BBC remained unchanged—*Yvonne pense toujours à l'heureuse occasion*—Le Cornec and his group in Plouha decided that, for security reasons, evading airmen should not be brought to Brittany until an evacuation operation was imminent. In Paris, however, the number of downed Allied aviators had reached the point where they began to overreach the capacity of the safe houses. Paul Campinchi urged Dumais to arrange for some of them to be transferred to Brittany.

In early January, outfitted in French peasant clothing and carrying their fake ID and *Ausweis* (coastal travel permit) documents, sixteen men, divided into groups of twos and threes, boarded a train at the Gare Montparnasse railway station in Paris with guides who would escort them as far as St. Brieuc. There, the evacuees would be turned over to local Resistance members, and their guides would return immediately to Paris.

USAAF pilot First Lieutenant Richard Smith was among the airmen on that first train. His B-17 had been attacked by seven German fighters on its return from a successful bombing raid on Ludwigshafen on December 30, 1943, and he and his crew had bailed out near the French town of St. Just-en-Chaussée, 60 miles north of Paris. Smith had been wounded, but less seriously than two of his colleagues who were taken to a hospital after landing; another was killed when his parachute failed to open. According to Smith's evacuation report (dictated to MI-9 after his return to London), he and three other members of his crew—Second Lieutenant William Booher, Technical Sergeant Alphonse Mele, and Staff Sergeant Jerry Eshius—landed successfully in a field. A group of French farm workers identified them as Americans and hurried them away to several nearby houses where they were given food and civilian clothes. Instructed to remain very quiet, Smith and his companions remained hidden for nine days, after which they were taken by car to Paris where they stayed for two days in the house of an English-speaking woman. Their photos were taken for ID papers, and they were questioned at length by three people—"Captain Hamilton" (Dumais), a larger man who also spoke English, and an American-educated girl, "Claudette." After "Hamilton" was satisfied with the men's responses—confirming that they were indeed who they claimed to be—"Claudette" outlined the arrangements for their transfer to the coastal region of Brittany. They would travel in the company of other airmen, and all would be escorted by guides. They were warned to keep their mouths shut, not to smoke (since Americans held their cigarettes differently from the French), not to make eye contact with each other or anyone else, and to feign deep sleep to avoid having to reply if they were spoken to by an official.

The first leg of the journey was the 250 miles (400 kilometers) west by train to St. Brieuc. Upon their arrival, Smith and his fifteen companions filed onto the platform. Wordlessly, the Paris guides turned their "packages" over to their Breton colleagues who carried German newspapers conspicuously under one arm as a means of recognition. A *gendarme* at the station checked everybody's papers, but waved the airmen on.

Owing to their numbers, some of the airmen were dispersed among families in St. Brieuc. Others were put aboard the small local train to Plouha. For the Shelburne operations, the branch line to Plouha was highly convenient. However, for reasons unrelated to the evacuations, the Germans canceled the train service the following month, requiring that alternative forms of transport to Plouha be found. Smith, Booher and two other men traveled on the train, however, and were escorted to Plouha by a young woman, Marie-Thérèse Le Calvez, whose mother hid the men in their house upon arrival. Madame Le Calvez was a widow who would ultimately lose four of her five sons in the war. Her daughter, Marie-Thérèse—the "Yvonne" of the BBC messages—was a remarkable 19 year-old who worked as a secretary at the local Agricultural Association and was to become one of the Shelburne Line's most valuable operatives. Marie-Thérèse participated as a guide in all of the Bonaparte evacuations. She and her mother also hid a number of airmen in their house between operations.

Smith's colleagues in the Le Calvez house, besides Booher, were Americans also. They were top turret gunner Sergeant Walter Sentkoski and tail gunner Sergeant James King. Both men had been in hiding for some months.

Sentkoski's plane had gone down in a bombing raid over Douai, on the northeastern coast of France, on August 15, 1943. As he bailed out, he recalled the instructions given by MI-9 in his pre-mission briefing: "Go into immediate hiding. Stay that way for the first few days."

He fell to the ground in a field and began taking off his parachute. As he did this, a nearby group of French workers scattered. Sentkoski left his chute in a heap near a haystack and hid behind a barn. Moments later a car stopped and Sentkoski heard loud German voices, obviously asking questions. Soon afterward, the car drove off and a farmer appeared with a bag holding the sergeant's chute and flying equipment, weighted down with a huge brick. Using sign language, the Frenchman made Sentkoski understand that he should move on and drop the bag into a nearby canal.

Walking for several nights and sleeping during the day, Sentkoski came across a second farmer who was happy to learn the stranger was American and turned him over to the Underground. The rest of his "journey" was arranged so that Sentkoski never knew exactly where he was until his arrival in Paris. There, he underwent intensive questioning of the sort to which Lt. Smith and his crewmen had been subjected. Dumais insisted on it. For the security of both the Shelburne Line and the evacuation operations, they had to be sure the airmen were indeed who they claimed to be.

Sergeant King's plane had gone down in flames over northeastern France the previous August. He parachuted out and managed to land behind a high hedge that gave him immediate cover. He doffed his chute and tossed away his helmet and throat microphone. Moments later, hearing Germans approach, he climbed into a haystack. Of his ten-member crew, King was the only lucky one. Six men went down with the plane; three were captured by Germans upon landing.

After dark, King checked the mini-compass in his escape kit and set off southward, walking all night. At daybreak, he encountered a farmer who gave him food and civilian clothing and invited him to spend the night. In the farmhouse that evening, King lit an American-made cigarette from a packet in his flight jacket. Instantly, the farmer yanked it out of his hand, doused it and, holding his nose, cried *"Les Boches! Les Boches!"*— the pejorative term for Germans. King realized that something as simple as the odor of his cigarettes, which differed from that of the strong-smelling French Gauloises, could betray him.

Early the next morning the farmer sent King on his way with a packet of food. After numerous detours King found another house where a man handed him a note written in English. The man disappeared immediately, but the note said, "Don't be afraid. Stay here until 5 p.m." That night at dark, King was picked up by a Resistance member and for the next six months his "journey," too, was arranged. Transferred from house to house in dizzying succession, he knew little about his surroundings until he eventually arrived with Smith and the others in Plouha.

Months later, during his interrogation by MI-9 in London, King, like all evacuees, was asked what advice he would give to other downed aviators.[1] "Do everything the people tell you," he wrote. "Before making contact, do not walk along canals or train tracks even when they are in the country for they are patrolled at all times."

Sentkowski, who was several years older than King, wrote: "Avoid the prosperous homes—if you see new and expensive laundry hanging from

---

1 In their post-evacuation reports to MI-9 about their experiences in France, including their transfers from place to place, each man recalled details they had observed, as well as information their rescuers had given them. Sentkoski reported that, at the end of December 1943, Allied bombers had damaged the ball-bearing plant in Paris and that he, himself, saw the wreckage of the Renault factory in Paris which had been subject to heavy bombardments by both the British and Americans. The fact that the men were not allowed to carry any personal effects or notes with them attests to their excellent powers of observation and memory.

clothesline avoid that house; seek aid from the humble. Patience is the prime requisite."

Lieutenant Smith's advice was equally succinct: "Do what the French tell you to do. Don't ask questions. Don't be untrusting of the French!"

As the January storms continued and the BBC radioed that Yvonne was "still thinking about the happy occasion," the families in Brittany who had agreed to house the airmen from Paris began to run low on provisions. The men themselves had no idea what sacrifices their hosts were making to find food. Meat, cheese, milk, cream, real coffee and chocolate were impossible to find except on the black market, and only by those who had the cash. Although families with gardens were better off, they still had to scrounge to supplement the menus for their hungry "guests." Throughout the war years, the average French intake of calories was estimated to be the second lowest in Western Europe. The extra mouths of the aviators posed an additional burden.

To ease the situation, the men housed in St. Brieuc were moved out of the city and placed with families in the countryside outside Plouha. Everybody awaited the "green light," though for security reasons Dumais and Labrosse remained the only ones who knew the BBC sentence codes. The two French-Canadians had remained in Paris, but finally, in mid-January, they were ordered back to Plouha by Room 900 to set up their "command center." In Le Cornec's café, near Plouha's town square, Labrosse set up his radio. Testing it, he sent a message to MI-9 confirming that he and Dumais had arrived safely.

A week later, at 7 p.m. on January 28, 1944, the two men turned on the shortwave. The radio crackled with static as Labrosse adjusted the dial to the BBC frequency. While they waited, a series of coded messages came first over the airwaves. Then—*Bonjour tout le monde à la Maison d'Alphonse.* These were the words Dumais and Labrosse had been waiting for—the go-ahead signal for the first *Opération Bonaparte.* The two men felt like shouting. At last, two months after their arrival in France in the Lysander, they were about to embark on their true mission. They hid their excitement as best they could so as not to draw the attention of the other people in the café, and also to conceal from Le Cornec which of the messages had been intended for them. Le Cornec knew from their broad smiles at the end of the broadcast, however, that the mission was on. The three men drank a toast: "To success and a busy season."

Dumais and Labrosse listened to the BBC again at 9 p.m. for a second message indicating that a Royal Navy Motor Gun Boat (MGB) had departed Dartmouth, England. The crossing would take four to five hours, and after receiving the appropriate confirmation message, the two French-Canadians rushed out to alert the local guides who would escort the airmen to the beach. From one side of Plouha to the other passed the whispered message, "Pick up your 'packages' immediately and take them to the *Maison d'Alphonse*. The MGB has left Dartmouth."

Jean and Mimi Gicquel had moved into the *Maison d'Alphonse* several weeks before. They had furnished the cottage sparsely and prepared it as a safe house. The windows in the attic, where the airmen would be hidden on the evenings of the evacuations, were covered with heavy black fabric to prevent light seeping out. The path to Anse Cochat, which Dumais and Labrosse had examined in December with Le Cornec, lay directly across the road from the cottage. No other houses in the vicinity could be seen.

On the night of the first Bonaparte operation, Marie-Thérèse Le Calvez escorted Smith, Booher, Sentkoski and King the mile from her house to the *Maison d'Alphonse*. At the same time, other guides collected men from other safe houses, leading them silently across muddy farm fields, through hedges and ditches and finally, into the dimly lit cottage. Smith reported that a "crowd" of other men awaited his group up in the attic.

Around 10:30 p.m., Dumais arrived and delivered a briefing to the sixteen airmen—thirteen Americans, three RAF—who were squeezed together under the cottage roof. There was also a Russian ("Ivan"), and two young Frenchmen who were on the run from the Gestapo. Smith and others knew Dumais from Paris as "Captain Hamilton." François Le Cornec knew him only as "Léon." That night, Dumais invented yet another name for himself, while some of the airmen, who had become used to sign language from the French, were surprised to hear English spoken without an accent.

"Good evening," Dumais began. "My name is Captain Harrison. I'm a member of the British Intelligence Service, and I'm here to help you get back to England."

He spoke in a voice that was quiet but firm. "This is the last lap of your long journey. It is the last, but the most dangerous one. We are about a mile from the English Channel; if everything goes well, you'll be aboard a British warship in two hours and in England by nine o'clock in the morning."

This news caused a murmur of excitement among the airmen, but Dumais silenced them. "All other rescue lines have been infiltrated; many French helpers have suffered horrifying torture at the hands of the Gestapo to force disclosure of names, routes and safe houses. Many have died or committed suicide to guard against betraying their compatriots or families. I will not have this operation put at risk by a foolish slip of the tongue."

As he said this, Dumais was undoubtedly thinking about Val Williams, his impetuous MI-9 predecessor, who had escaped from the French prison in which he had been incarcerated and was downstairs in the *Maison d'Alphonse* at that very moment, literally beneath Dumais' feet. The reason Williams was not in the attic with the others was that he had a broken leg, but he was on the list of men to be evacuated from Anse Cochat—much to Dumais' extreme irritation, as his first encounter with the man earlier that evening had been disagreeable.

As with everything Williams did, his escape story, too, had been larger than life. Following his arrest *en route* to Spain the previous June, Williams was sent first to Frèsnes prison, south of Paris, and later transferred to Rennes. There, he befriended a Russian prison guard, "Ivan," whom Williams promised to take with him to England if Ivan could help him break out. The two made their escape in December 1943, although Williams broke his leg jumping into a moat from the outer wall of the prison. Ivan helped Williams hobble to a hiding place and with the aid of a local farmer they made their way to a Resistance safe house, where a sympathetic doctor put Williams' leg in a cast. Paul Campinchi arranged for their train travel to Paris by paying two *gendarmes* to escort Williams and Ivan in handcuffs as "prisoners." Campinchi asked Dumais to schedule their evacuation as soon as possible. Dumais agreed, but he was not pleased about this additional burden. He was concerned that the Shelburne operation would be compromised by Williams' recklessness.

Airey Neave, in Room 900, wanted Williams out of France as soon as possible for the same reason.

After hearing the first BBC message, Dumais went to the house in Plouha where Williams was being hidden to brief him about his transfer to *Maison d'Alphonse* and Anse Cochat. Dumais found the man reclining in an easy chair in his host's living room, his plastered leg on a footstool. He had glass of wine in his hand and was bragging that he'd be back in England by the next morning.

Furious, Dumais pulled out his pistol in front of the host, pointed it at Williams and told him not to utter another word, or he'd be a dead man.

Now, in the attic, visibly heated as he spoke to the airmen, Dumais told them, "No one will move or speak until I give the order to do so. Before we go downstairs, tell me your name. I also need you to hand over your IDs, any money you're carrying, and anything else personal that could betray the operation."

A voice at the back spoke up. "We don't have to give you anything, just our rank and serial number. You don't need to know our names."

"You take orders from me," Dumais said, pronouncing each word slowly and forcefully. "I'm the one who decides what you take with you. You'll do what I tell you to do, or you'll return to England with a hole in your belly."

There was no doubt that "Captain Harrison" meant business. His threat to shoot anyone who made a sound was real. Thereafter, no one talked back—and Dumais reassured them that their dogtags, money and so forth would be returned to them on the boat.

Dumais continued his instructions, telling the men that when they exited the *Maison d'Alphonse* they would meet the guides and form a single-file line. "You are to take hold of the next person's jacket with your left hand and not let go under any circumstances until you reach the cliff at Anse Cochat." He described the terrain they would cover on their way to the evacuation beach—the "tunnel" of brambles, the muddy farmlands, the Customs path they would cross, then the cliff, and the descent.

"We cross an area patrolled by the enemy," he told them, "and the slightest sound can reveal us. If we encounter any sentries along the path, be ready to tighten ranks and fight by any means—hands, feet, body, teeth. The guides and I have pistols. If you have a knife, use it."

The cliff was the most dangerous part of the operation. Almost vertical and about 100 feet high, it was composed of scree—sharp, jagged, loose rock. As the group reached the edge of the cliff, each aviator was to let go of the person in front and wait in line. When the guide gave the signal, the first person was to lie down on his back, keep his legs extended but separate, and try to dig his heels into the loose rock to prevent too rapid a descent.

"Your butt will hurt like hell," Dumais said, "and the person above you may dislodge some rocks; but whatever you do, don't . . . make . . . a sound."

"Two of the guides will descend before you can begin," he continued. "Yvonne" (Marie-Thérèse Le Calvez) will go first, stationed at the base with a flashlight; "Job" (Joseph Mainguy), will go second and remain halfway down the cliff with a flashlight signaling to the MGB by Morse Code. "Tarzan" (Pierre Huet) will remain at the top."

One of the airmen asked, dubiously, if Yvonne was a woman.

"Don't worry," Dumais replied. "She's one of our best guides."

Dumais added that one of the evacuees—Williams—would have to be carried on a litter. Dumais did not name him, but said, "Do not talk to this guy. Ignore him totally."

"I will be the first into the water to meet the sailors who need to unload some heavy bags first," he continued. "Wait for the sailors to help you into the boat. Do not attempt to climb in by yourself."

Then, before leading the airmen downstairs from the attic, he repeated the procedure for descending the cliff and explained where they would be grouped along the base of the cliff while awaiting the surfboats.

"And remember…" Dumais stopped, motioned them to stand up and follow him and, looking severely at each man, he repeated, "From now on, not one word."

It was 11:30 p.m. as the men filed out of the *Maison d'Alphonse* and into the dark where six guides were waiting—Le Cornec, Mainguy, Huet, Le Calvez, and two others, Francis Baudet and Jean Tréhiou. Three additional men waited with a hand-made stretcher for Val Williams. Job Mainguy, Marie-Thérèse and Huet would take the lead. Dumais would bring up the

The tunnel of brambles.

The cliff.

rear behind the men carrying Williams, who was strapped to the litter and, for once, made no sound.

The line formed, crossed the road from the house and headed east along the thorny path, then across the Customs path and to the top of the cliff.

Smith, Booher, Sentkowski and King—who had all been hidden in the Le Calvez house—were sure they had covered at least five miles on foot by that time. One by one, seconds apart, the three RAF airmen, sixteen Americans, and Ivan the Russian, began their descent. Rocks came loose and tumbled down, smacking the head of the person below. No one let out a sound, until it was Val Williams' turn, but the sound of the far-out surf muffled his moans as he slid and bounced abruptly downhill, still tightly strapped to his makeshift litter.

Grouped into the cave the men kneeled or sat down to wait. One hour passed, then two. The tide began to rise. What was taking so long? Had something gone wrong? More than one man longed to ask how long they were supposed to remain in their hiding place, but their French guides said nothing, and the airmen waited on in silence. In the meantime, Job Mainguy, his red flashlight covered by a cardboard tube, flashed the Morse code signal "B" repeatedly out to sea at one minute intervals waiting—hoping—for a response.

Don Douglass at the entrance to one of the caves at Anse Cochat.

DUMAIS' SHELBURNE TEAM

Dumais, Lucien (code name "Léon"): Shelburne Line chief organizer

Labrosse, Raymond ("Claude"): Shelburne's Radioman and Dumais' partner.

Paris:
Campinchi, Paul ("François"): agent responsible for finding safe houses, printing false IDs, interrogating aviators, and delivering *"colis"* ("packages" of airmen) to Brittany.

Plouha:
Le Cornec, François: chief of the Plouha Resistance group; owner of a café/butcher shop.

Baudet, Francis: Shelburne agent; brother-in-law of Guiguite Le Saux.

Gicquel, Jean & Mimi (Marie): Shelburne agents, owners of the *Maison d'Alphonse*, where the airmen were housed just prior to each evacuation.

Huet, Pierre ("Tarzan"): Shelburne agent and guide; former military pilot.

Le Calvez, Marie-Therese ("Yvonne"): 19-year-old Shelburne guide and agent; secretary at the Agricultural Association.

Le Saux Pierre, Marguerite (Guiguite): 17 years old; Baudet's young sister-in-law; good friend of Marie-Thérèse Le Calvez; could not participate in Shelburne until her 18th birthday.

Mainguy, Joseph ("Job"): Shelburne agent; Merchant Marine officer until outbreak of the War.

Tréhiou, Jean: Shelburne & FFI agent; French Naval officer.

Plouha Safe House providers (In all, seven households participated; only those listed below appear in the text.)
Le Calvez, Léonie: Widowed mother of Marie-Thérèse and five sons (four of whom were killed during the war).
Le Saux, Madame: mother of Guiguite; housed Labrosse & Dumais from time to time.
Ropers, Anne: she and her family housed Lt. Guy Hamilton & others.
Tréhiou, Marie: sister of Jean Tréhiou.

Guingamp agents:
Branchoux, Mathurin: Chief of the A.S. (*Armée Secrète*); chief Guingamp agent; potato dealer.
Le Cun, Georges: Shelburne Agent; member of the A.S.
Kérambrun, François: Shelburne Agent, garage owner and owner-driver of the truck that carried aviators to Plouha. During the day he used his truck working for the Germans. At night he worked for the Resistance.

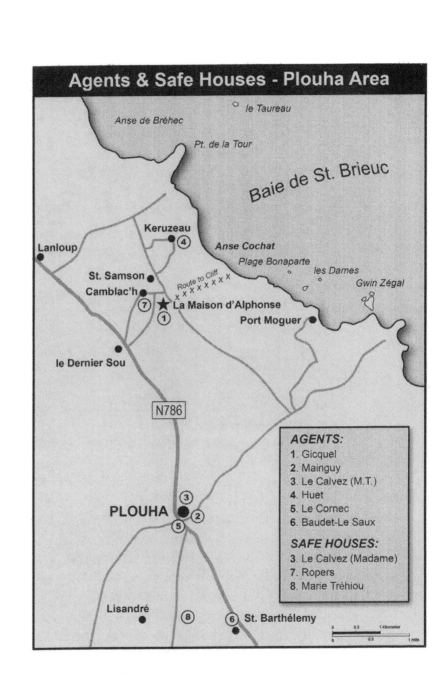

Agents & Safe Houses - Plouha Area

le Taureau

Anse de Bréhec

Pt. de la Tour

Baie de St. Brieuc

Keruzeau

④

Anse Cochat

Lanloup

Plage Bonaparte

les Dames

Gwin Zégal

St. Samson

Route to Cliff
x x x x x x x x x x

Camblac'h

⑦ ★ La Maison d'Alphonse

①

Port Moguer

le Dernier Sou

N786

③

PLOUHA ●

②

⑤

Lisandré

⑧

⑥ St. Barthélemy

AGENTS:
1. Gicquel
2. Mainguy
3. Le Calvez (M.T.)
4. Huet
5. Le Cornec
6. Baudet-Le Saux

SAFE HOUSES:
3. Le Calvez (Madame)
7. Ropers
8. Marie Tréhiou

0   0.5   1 kilometer
0   0.5   1 mile

CHAPTER 4

MOONLESS SORTIES
MGB 503
"THE CROSS-CHANNEL TRAIN"

On the morning of the first scheduled Bonaparte operation, Lieutenant
Michael Marshall, of the Royal Navy's 15th Motor Gun Boat Flotilla, and
his navigator, Lieutenant David Birkin, disembarked from a London train
at Dartmouth, on the southwest coast of England. Marshall had played
rugby for both Oxford and England before the war, and served with
distinction in covert coastal operations with the Royal Navy Volunteer
Reserve. In November 1943, the Navy appointed him master of the
15th Flotilla's newest and fastest Motor Gun Boat, MGB 503. Birkin,
who was the Flotilla's navigation officer, would participate in the first of
the Bonaparte evacuation operations, although subsequently he served
aboard the 503's sister ship MGB 502.

From the Dartmouth railway station, the two men headed directly
to the port, where, in an old paddle-steamer used by the Flotilla as
a base, they met their ship's crew and began a briefing that covered
intelligence reports, photographic reconnaissance, and any additional
details related to their mission that night—a mission that would be the
first of the *Opérations Bonaparte* carried out by the Shelburne Line.
Some of the information presented in the briefing pertained to enemy
shipping movements in the English Channel over the past 24-hours
and had been obtained from German naval reports transmitted in codes
generated by German ENIGMA machines. Though the codes changed

A German ENIGMA machine

daily, the British were able to read the reports as a result of the top-secret wartime code-breaking efforts at Bletchley Park, sixty miles northwest of London, by some of England's finest mathematical intellects. The Germans remained unaware of this, and even in Britain, details of the intelligence work undertaken at Bletchley Park and the breaking of the ENIGMA code remained secret until the 1970s.

The 15th Motor Gun Boat Flotilla had been established in 1942 to support special cross-Channel operations between France and England. The first boats used for the early missions were slow and cumbersome, but by January 1944, two much improved models of aggressive state-of-the-art design were working the coast of Brittany. One—MGB 502, dispatched from Falmouth—delivered and picked up agents along the north coast of Brittany and supplied the French Resistance with intelligence and war supplies. The second—MGB 503, based in Dartmouth—was assigned to pick up and return to England Allied airmen shot down over Western Europe who had either evaded or escaped from the enemy. MGB 503 was the ultimate key to the eight Shelburne Line evacuation operations, eventually earning the moniker "Cross-Channel Train" for its numerous successful crossings.

In size, shape and speed, the wooden-hulled MGB 503 resembled the PT (Patrol Torpedo) boats used by the US Navy. Equipped with three powerful diesel engines, it measured 117 feet (35 meters) in length; had a beam of 20 feet 3 inches (6 m); a shallow draft of 4 feet 1 inch (1.2 m); a displacement of 95 tons; a sum total of 3000 brake horsepower (bhp), and a maximum speed of 28 knots (over 30 miles per hour). It was one of the fastest boats for its size.

Early in the war, the masters (captains) of the MGBs had determined

Motor Gun Boat 503 underway.

that a solid black hull was visible during moonless operations and stood out far too much during twilight to be safe. Therefore it was decided to paint the upper part of the hull a rosy-orange above the waterline to camouflage it, and dark blue near the waterline, rendering the vessel practically invisible before sunrise or after sunset—the most dangerous times. This unique camouflage was critical for inshore operations in enemy territory. In summer, this meant the vessels had to be away from the Breton coast by approximately 2:00 a.m., before Nautical Twilight began at that latitude (48°40'N) and the horizon became distinguishable.[1] In the winter months, the timing was more flexible. In all instances, it was essential that operations be conducted on moonless nights.

Although their shallow draft allowed them to navigate near the Channel coastal platform, the MGBs rolled extensively in heavy seas— sometimes close to the point of capsizing. The 503's navigator, David Birkin, fought acute seasickness, since his station aboard the vessel was a small, enclosed space beneath the bridge. His equipment included a compass, a Radio Direction Finder (RDF), nautical paper charts, nautical almanac, parallel rules, dividers, pencils and various other small

---

1 For any given latitude, the Nautical Almanac defines Civil Twilight as the period when the sun is 6° below the horizon and objects are clearly distinguishable. Nautical Twilight is defined as the time when the center of the sun is 12° below the horizon and objects become discernible along the horizon. *National Weather Service.*

navigation tools. As navigator, Birkin had to continuously estimate the force of the wind, monitor the tide, calculate the velocity of the current and allow for any margin of error. He then had to plot this data on the chart. A navigation error of as little as two degrees could create an error in eventual position of as much as five degrees. Birkin performed his job expertly even as the vessel rolled continuously from side to side, tossing him and his equipment violently around in his "cage" during the crossings of the rough English Channel.

On clear nights, the sailors above deck worried that the ship's wake would create phosphorescence that could easily be detected by the Germans. This glowing condition occurred in water of moderate depths (10 to 20 fathoms) as a result of the disturbance of microscopic sea creatures. Fortunately, most of the Channel crossings took place in unsettled weather, when surface chop masked the glow created by the ship's propellers.

Shipboard noise was also a security issue, especially close to shore. To avoid the slightest sound while anchoring, hemp fiber rather than steel chain was used for the 503's anchor line. In addition, the rollers, chocks and cleats were covered in black canvas—again to cut down noise.

A further concern for the men of MGB 503 was the fact that the Germans operated a coast-watching radar station 16 kilometers (10 miles) to the north of Anse Cochat. However, the wooden hull of the MGB made it harder to detect, and the numerous offshore rocks around the proposed anchoring location also rendered it somewhat inconspicuous.

On deck, MGB 503 carried from two to four wooden surfboats, depending on the number of evacuees for a particular operation. Each surfboat carried two oarsmen and a coxswain (steersman), all experienced in covert operations. An MI-9 official also occupied a place in one of the boats. For the Bonaparte operations, this was Airey Neave's Room 900 partner, Patrick Windham-Wright.

The MGB surfboats were a 14-foot clinker design—i.e., their hulls were constructed from overlapping planks—which gave maximum strength for the least weight. They were double-ended, with a blunt bow and stern, and an oarlock for a steering oar to facilitate maneuvering from either end and to keep the boat from turning sideways to the waves and broaching when surfing into shore. When the surfboat hit the beach, the coxswain switched to the other end with his steering oar. That way, the bow of the boat automatically faced the surf, ready to head back into the waves without the boat having to be turned around. Rubbing strakes (hard rubber strips) running along the sides of the surfboat helped deaden noise. To decrease visibility, the four oars of each small boat, as well as its oarlocks, were covered with black canvas.

For each of the Bonaparte operations, MGB 503 left Dartmouth between 4 p.m. and 6 p.m. and headed out to the lighthouse at Start Point, their navigational point of departure. From here, they set a course of 4 degrees east, navigating thereafter by dead reckoning—calculating their position at regular intervals by estimating the direction and distance traveled. Depending on sea conditions, the crossing was expected to take about six hours each way. At 40 nautical miles[2] from the Breton coast, echo soundings provided an indication that they had reached Hurd Deep (*Fosse Centrale*)—a trench 70 nautical miles long by 2 nautical miles wide—enabling Marshall and Birkin to confirm their position. Although their vessel carried radar, it was not used for fear that its signal would alert the enemy patrolling the Channel and French coast.

About 15 nautical miles from their objective off the beach at Anse Cochat, MGB 503 reduced its speed to 10 knots and used its engine exhaust silencers. At eight nautical miles from the coast, the vessel cut across the route used by German convoys, again reducing speed and proceeding in total blackness. No lights of any kind were permitted, except by Birkin, wedged below, who used a dim red light to read his charts and make notations. As they reached the shallow coastal plateau, Marshall paid strict attention to the depth sounder and the charted depths to verify key checkpoints along the route. Not only was it critical to find the right beach—Bonaparte—but the entire section of coast was dangerous and difficult to navigate, with strong currents and hidden rock outcroppings everywhere.

Sighting *Le Grand Léjon*—a lighthouse 15 nautical miles east of Pointe de la Tour—Marshall changed the vessel's course, shutting down

---

2 A nautical mile (nm) is a unit of distance based on approximately one minute of arc of latitude. Its International established length is 6,076 feet (1,852 meters) compared to a Statute mile (land mile) that is equal to 5,280 feet (1,609 meters).

two of its engines and slowing to about 4 knots. Two nautical miles from shore, in a depth of 6.5 fathoms (12 meters), he cut the third engine and the MGB drifted to a stop naturally. The rocks on a hand drawing made by Job Mainguy of *Le Taureau*—the rock off Pointe de la Tour—and those shown on the chart played a critical part in determining the exact anchoring position. The anchor would not be dropped, however, until the faint red flashes of the Morse code letter "B," for Bonaparte (— . . . / dash dot dot dot), repeated at one-minute intervals, were seen coming from the shore.

Once MGB 503 arrived in position, Marshall gave the order to anchor, keeping the MGB's bow pointed directly toward Pointe de la Tour, so that just its narrowest profile showed. The distance to the pillboxes on the point was less than one nautical mile (1500 meters) from the vessel.

As soon as the anchor held, an order was whispered to lower the surfboats. For the first mission there were three surfboats manned by a total of nine crewmen plus Windham-Wright. The boats were slipped silently into the water and rowed toward shore. As camouflage, each man had blackened his face and any exposed skin. Marshall and the rest of his crew remained at their combat stations in the meantime, ready to make a quick get-away in case of emergency or an attack.

On shore, as the anxious evacuees watched and waited on the beach, they could see the glow of cigarettes smoked by sentries on guard at the pillboxes on Pointe de la Tour just to the west. Suddenly, just as the tide began to change, three small black specks became discernible, approaching through the surf. As the specks turned into boats, Dumais waded out to greet them, with Le Cornec and Huet behind him. Each man carried a pistol. The men in the boats were armed with submachine guns.

"Dinan," Dumais said softly to the one-armed man in the lead boat. This had been the agreed-upon password.

"St Brieuc," Windham-Wright uttered—correctly—in reply.

The guns were put away, and Dumais conversed with Windham-Wright while Le Cornec and the others unloaded from the boats a 30-liter tank of gasoline and six waterproof suitcases packed with supplies. Finally, the waiting airmen, plus Williams, Ivan, and the two young Frenchmen, were brought forward from the beach and loaded aboard. The total time

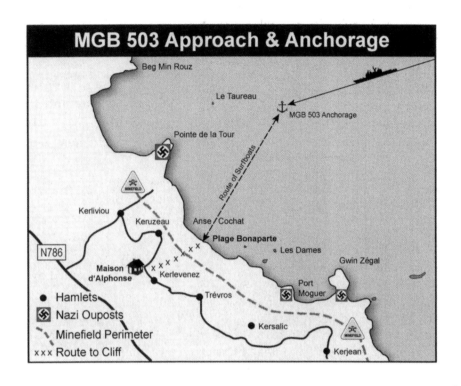

MGB 503 Approach & Anchorage

Beg Min Rouz

Le Taureau

MGB 503 Anchorage

Pointe de la Tour

Route of Surfboats

MINEFIELD

Kerliviou

Keruzeau

Anse Cochat

Plage Bonaparte

Les Dames

Gwin Zégal

N786

Maison d'Alphonse

Kerlevenez

Trévros

Port Moguer

Kersalic

MINEFIELD

Kerjean

- ● Hamlets
- Nazi Ouposts
- ‐ ‐ Minefield Perimeter
- x x x Route to Cliff

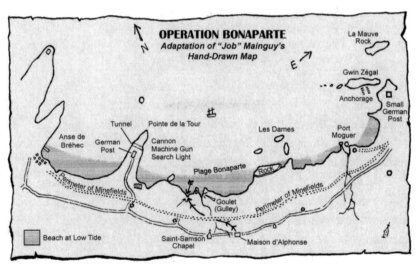

OPERATION BONAPARTE
Adaptation of "Job" Mainguy's Hand-Drawn Map

N

E

La Mauve Rock

Gwin Zégal

Anchorage

Small German Post

Tunnel

Pointe de la Tour

Les Dames

Port Moguer

Anse de Bréhec

German Post

Cannon Machine Gun Search Light

Plage Bonaparte

Rock

Perimeter of Minefields

Perimeter of Minefields

Goulet (Gulley)

Beach at Low Tide

Saint-Samson Chapel

Maison d'Alphonse

for the operation was twenty-five minutes. This was too slow for Dumais' comfort, but everything had gone without incident. The MGB did not appear to have been picked up on German radar, and the transfers of both men and supplies had proceeded without difficulty.

The men in the boats bid *au revoir* to Dumais and the others and rowed back out through the surf.

On the beach, the tide was rising rapidly. Dumais and his fellow guides, soaked by the waves, slid and slipped across the cobbles to begin their ascent up the cliff, dragging with them the heavy canvas suitcases and the tank of gasoline. Marie-Thérèse Le Calvez worked as hard as the men, taking one of the cases herself and laboriously lugging it up the scree-slope.

Within forty-five minutes the group was back in the *Maison d'Alphonse,* where they had hot coffee and cognac. Dumais was elated that the operation had gone off smoothly, but as he later wrote in a memoir, *The Man Who Went Back,* because of this he made "a silly mistake," opening the suitcases in front of everybody. In the cases were weapons, ammunition, a wireless set for Labrosse, chocolate, cigarettes, coffee, whiskey—everything Dumais had asked for. One suitcase contained four million francs, packaged in tight bundles of worn 10,000 franc bills. This money was to pay the Shelburne operatives and cover their expenses, but while he examined it Dumais felt what he described as "an air of expectancy" around him.

Dumais had already discussed with Le Cornec how much he would give to each person, and they had been paid accordingly, "but seeing all this money they imagined I was going to dish it out by the fistful." No one, Dumais included, believed the guides or host families were being paid adequately for the risks they were taking, but he didn't want anybody working just for the money—and paying too much had its own dangers. As Dumais put it, "Some people lose their heads when they get a bit of money, start drinking heavily, and then start talking. In addition, if a number of people in a small town suddenly appeared flush, the word would quickly get around and suspicions might be aroused."

The situation was defused, in any case. Dumais distributed some of the luxuries to the others, gave the arms to Le Cornec to hide, and took the money to the Le Calvez house, where Marie-Thérèse's mother offered him yet more coffee and cognac. He stayed there for the night and would later write that the house was warm and plenty of blankets covered his bed, but for a long time afterwards he could still feel the bitter chill of the water.

In the meantime, as they reached the MGB, the airmen and the crews from the three surfboats climbed aboard the larger vessel with the aid of rope scrambling nets. Lieutenant Marshall gave the order to weigh anchor, with the hemp line passed hand over hand, and the homeward voyage began under the power of a single, muffled engine. The three surfboats were towed astern. Only when Marshall judged they were sufficiently offshore was everything properly stowed, and only after they had passed *Le Grand Léjon* did the MGB power up to full speed.

For the airmen below the vessel's deck, this was finally their chance to speak out loud. Excitedly they exchanged rescue stories, and talked about their experiences of the past few days. Smith, Booher, Stenkoski and King—all of whom had hidden at the Le Calvez house—had known Marie-Thérèse Le Calvez by name, but most of the airmen had no idea of the real identities of those who had participated in their rescue, nor did they know the name *Shelburne Line*. They thought only that they had benefited from exceptionally good luck—which was true, in its way—and most remained only dimly aware of the extreme risks undertaken by their hosts, guides, MI-9 agents and the crew of the small British naval vessel now ferrying them to safety.

Six hours later, as MGB 503 approached the coast of England, the sound and sight of RAF Spitfires and Hurricanes filled the air and the vessel was escorted into Dartmouth Bay. The airmen disembarked and were sent directly to London by train. Following lengthy interrogation by MI-9 agents, they were released to their respective air bases scattered around England. Some fortunate U.S. airmen were sent home on leave.

The two young French men were shipped to "Patriotic School" in London where they, too, underwent intense interrogation. After verification of their loyalty to General De Gaulle, they and others were selected for either the Free French Forces (FFL) or French Forces of the

Interior (FFI).[3]

As for Val Williams, his return to England marked the end of what Airey Neave described as his "picturesque career" in Occupied France. He was subjected to a lengthy debriefing, during which he argued that although he was known to Gestapo personnel in southern France and Brittany, he could operate in other regions of the country. Neave disagreed, considering him a security risk anywhere in France. Williams was disappointed, but Neave acknowledged him as having laid much of the groundwork for the escape route from the Côte d'Armor to Dartmouth. Dumais was less generous, informing Room 900 that if they were to send Williams back to France, Dumais would shoot the man "on sight, personally."

Meanwhile, in Dartmouth Harbor, the tired sailors aboard MGB 503 refueled, restocked and cleaned their vessel in preparation for the next *Opération Bonaparte* sortie, whenever the weather promised another moonless night and MI-9 sent the order.

---

3 *Forces Françaises Libres*—known as FFL—was established in June 1940, when De Gaulle called on the French to continue to fight against Germany; the FFL joined forces with the Allies. FFI—*Forces Françaises de l'Intérieur*—was conceived in December 1943 to aid existing Resistance groups in France with arms, money, and strategies for sabotage.

CHAPTER 5

OPÉRATION BONAPARTE II
FEBRUARY 26-27, 1944

The first *Opération Bonaparte* had been a complete success, and Dumais saw no reason why it shouldn't be repeated—particularly as the number of Allied aviators awaiting evacuation from France continued to grow. Room 900 considered that the maximum number of men who could be evacuated during any one operation was twenty, or three to each of the Plouha guides. However, by February, more than thirty aviators were waiting to be sent to Brittany from Paris. Some of them had been hidden for weeks and they were bored and impatient. Their host families, who were running low on food, hoped the orders to send their "guests" to Brittany would come soon. In the meantime, they did their best to provide entertainment. They dug out playing cards; they spirited the men out at night for exercise; they scrounged for cigarettes on the black market. Every indulgence on the part of the French families required creativity, money, and tremendous risk.

As Allied bombing raids escalated over Germany and the west coast of France, the SS and Gestapo increased their presence in Brittany. The French called this period *la guerre des nerfs* ("the war of nerves"), as the news teetered between hopeful and pessimistic. While the BBC's clandestine broadcasts gave hope that the Allies were gaining ground against Germany, Vichy's Director of Propaganda, Philippe Henriot, continued to depict the Resistance as "a horde of terrorists and communists" on the official government radio.[1] Germany was also demanding that France supply a million more men between the ages of sixteen to sixty to work in German factories. Unable to fulfill this demand, the Vichy government went so far as to extend the call to childless married women ages twenty-one to thirty-five.

During this time, Dumais and Labrosse learned that the Germans had commandeered the local train from St. Brieuc to Plouha, leaving the Shelburne operatives without a local means of transfer. Le Cornec was already working on the problem, however. He made contact with two underground agents in the Guingamp region, Georges Le Cun and Mathurin Branchoux, and asked them to locate safe houses and find a means of transporting airmen to Plouha. François Kérambrun, who owned a garage in Guingamp and delivered supplies for the Germans during the day, agreed to take on the mission of delivering men the 15 miles (23 kms) to Plouha at night, before the 9 p.m. curfew.

Kérambrun's cover story, in the event that he was stopped, was that the men in the back of his truck were Polish workmen needed for a "rush job" on the German coastal defenses. Kérambrun reportedly rationalized to himself that he could be shot for transporting two evaders, so he might just as well carry twenty. Fuel was not a problem as his truck ran on *gazogène*, a substance produced by a gas generator that was mounted on the rear of the vehicle and burned either wood or coal as its primary fuel.

Prior to the second Bonaparte operation, Kérambrun had been unaware that the Germans had begun construction work on a tank trap— akin to a "Texas" cattle gate with steel spikes—on the road between Guingamp and Plouha. The project was incomplete when Kérambrun and his "packages" came upon it, and the truck became stuck on a wooden strut. The 21 airmen in the back worked to lift it off before the curfew commenced, and managed to do so just as two *gendarmes* arrived on the scene. Kérambrun debated killing them, but decided instead to tell them the truth. Like most Bretons, the *gendarmes* were supportive of the Allied cause and allowed the truck to continue on its way. For the airmen it had been a heart-stopping experience, and they continued to talk about it all the way to Dartmouth on MGB 503.

1 Henriot was executed by the Resistance on June 28, 1944, in Paris.

An example of a gazogène-fueled vehicle, France, WWII.

MI-9 finally alerted Dumais and Labrosse that the second *Opération Bonaparte* would take place the night of February 26. Forty-eight hours before this, two men who purported to be aviators arrived by train in Guingamp. Their arrival had been expected, but the train was several hours late and no one had waited on the station platform to escort the men to a safe house. Their Paris guide departed on the return train, leaving them with little option but to head for a local bar, where their behavior caused consternation. One of the men spoke fluent French. The other spoke only English. Both became rapidly intoxicated. Suspecting that the two were Nazi agents, the owner of the bar notified Dumais immediately.

Dumais sent two armed underground agents to the bar to bring the men to him for questioning. The French-speaker, L.J. Harmel, claimed that he was a Belgian Flight Sergeant serving with the RAF and that his plane had been shot down two months earlier. He staggered along in a drunken stupor, mumbling that since no one had been at the train station to meet them, he and his companion had gone to the bar simply to look for a priest to assist them. "That's the way we do it in Belgium. We look for the priest to help us," he told Dumais.

His companion, USAAF Staff Sergeant Lee C. Gordon, had been MIA (missing in action) for a year. Shot down on a bombing raid over Germany, he was captured and taken to a *dulag* (transit camp). There, his refusal to answer questions and his assertions that Germany was *kaputt* (finished) earned him several weeks in solitary confinement. Transferred to *Stalag Luft* VIIA, a POW camp in Germany run by the Luftwaffe (German Air Force), he made his first attempt to escape. Recaptured, he escaped a second time but was caught again. His third escape attempt in October 1943 proved successful. By freight train and on foot, he managed to reach France in November and finally made contact with the Resistance.

Harmel had a fondness for alcohol, but Gordon who had barely survived on POW camp food, hadn't tasted a drop of hard liquor for over a year. In the Guingamp bar, it had gone straight to his head, leaving him nauseated and unable to walk a straight line.

When the agents delivered the two men to Dumais, he was furious. If they were who they claimed to be, their behavior had been both dangerous and inexcusable. To his hostess, he said, "Do you have a place in the garden where we can bury two dead bodies if needed?"

Understanding that the men might be spies, she replied without hesitation, "Yes."

Dumais handcuffed Harmel immediately and took Gordon to the cellar to be interrogated first.

"Where are your dog-tags?" Dumais demanded.

"The Germans took them," Gordon replied.

"What squadron were you with?"

"365th Bomb Squadron."

"You say you're American. Where are you from?"

"California."

"That's interesting. Your ID says you're Australian."

Dumais didn't wait for an explanation but went on with his questioning.

"What date was your plane shot down and where?"

"A year ago—February 26, 1943, over Wilhelmshaven."

"So where have you been for twelve months?" Dumais asked sarcastically, adding, "I warn you, if your answers prove false, I'll put a bullet through your head." Gordon felt as if the Gestapo had caught up with him—Dumais asked the same damn questions.

Sweating profusely, Gordon launched into his lengthy story: his capture after bailing out; his weeks in solitary confinement for refusal to answer questions; his eventual transfer to the Stalag Luft POW camp; his first escape; his recapture; his second escape and recapture. And then, how he exchanged identities with an Australian POW who was sympathetic to his escape plan; how he made his ultimate escape to Alsace; and his eventual encounter with a member of the French Resistance. Talking as fast as he could in his groggy state, he described with amazing precision the effects of the Allied bombings he observed as he crossed Germany, hoping these details might give him a chance with Dumais. Gordon was more frightened on this night than he'd been in his entire life. As the effects of the liquor wore off, all he wanted was something to eat and to be able to sleep. "I've come this far," he thought. "I hope to God this won't be the bloody end."

He went on to explain that he had been returned to Paris just a few weeks before from the Breton port of Douarnenez, after an attempt by boat to evacuate him along with seven other airmen, had failed. He paused and said, "I think I'd better mention something else." He told Dumais that he had been demoted from Tech Sergeant to Private on his base in England. "I wasn't very disciplined. I talked back to my officers. I was late returning to base a bunch of times, and I took a swing at an MP." He added that, in combat, his commander let him wear his three stripes. If the enemy caught him, as a sergeant he would receive better treatment in a POW camp. Gordon was, accordingly, a combat sergeant and a land-based private.

Dumais ended his interrogation abruptly. He had enough information now and believed the young man could not have invented such a story—the extraordinary escapes, the precise observations as he traveled from place to place, the confession as to his character.

"I'll be back later," Dumais told him. "Just remember what I said. We can check your story." He locked the cellar door and went upstairs to tell Labrosse to radio Room 900 for corroboration of Gordon's answers. If Room 900 responded positively, Gordon would be evacuated the following night, along with fifteen other Allied aviators.

While Harmel and Gordon slept off their inebriation, Labrosse received verification of Gordon's claims. Dumais' perception had proved correct. Gordon would be evacuated the next night.

Harmel's future was more problematic. The Belgian excused himself repeatedly for his previous night's behavior, but Dumais did not trust his responses. Harmel's lack of discipline had placed everyone in jeopardy and he seemed arrogantly oblivious to that fact. Dumais eventually decided he would send him back to England—but in handcuffs.

At 9:15 p.m. on the night of February 26, Labrosse tuned to the BBC and heard the phrase *"Bonjour Tout le Monde . . ."* This was the green light for the second evacuation operation from Bonaparte beach.

An additional coded message indicated that MGB 503 had left Dartmouth three hours earlier and was headed across the Channel. Dumais notified Le Cornec immediately and, from safe house to safe house, the message passed, "Tell the guides to bring their 'packages' to the *Maison d'Alphonse*." Dumais himself would lead Harmel and Gordon to the cottage.

Marie-Thérèse Le Calvez and her mother greeted the news with relief. For more than two weeks, they had hidden six aviators in their second floor room. The men remained in the attic most of the day and were allowed downstairs only after dark. Marie-Thérèse herself played the role of the house "watch dog"—sleeping on the floor by the front door. With a German military post a mere 500 feet away, such caution was essential. Marie-Thérèse couldn't help but wonder if her neighbors suspected anything. Everyone knew there was a 10,000-franc reward for turning in Allied aviators, but Marie-Thérèse knew her neighbors hated the Occupiers as much as she and her mother did, and she was confident they would never stoop to betrayal. When they met, the conversations were always about the weather and what bakery might possibly have bread that week. No one ever breathed a word about anything else.

Secrecy was not the only issue, however. Feeding their guests was an equally large problem. Germany was demanding ever more food from Breton farms, for little compensation. The year's wheat stores were almost depleted, and it was impossible to find bread in the markets. Russo-German conscripts pillaged chickens and rabbits from private homes, broke into houses, set fire to farms, and confiscated horses. The Vichy press attributed these crimes and the general lack of food to the Resistance *terroristes*.

Each day Marie-Thérèse scoured the Plouha countryside, looking for food and bargaining with farmers whose land had not been mined or otherwise rendered useless by the enemy. "I pretended that we had German workers at the house, but I wondered if the farmers were really fooled or if they were silently helping us," Marie-Thérèse later said. During the day, her mother bustled about the kitchen, trying to scrape up meals from what little fresh food they obtained and to distract the men she called her "impatient little ones."

When the go-ahead signal finally came, on February 26, the six aviators in the Le Calvez house were overcome with excitement and relief. Their next response was to race back upstairs to their hiding place in the attic and rummage through a trunkful of heavy clothes that had belonged to Marie-Thérèse's father. The February weather in Brittany was brutal. Temperatures had dropped dramatically, and the airmen would need whatever they could find in the attic trunk.

Then came the departure. This was a poignant moment, as Madame Le Calvez had become attached to her "little ones," and she embraced each young man tenderly. Though excited to be leaving at last, they returned her hugs, some of the men with tears rolling down their cheeks.

Marie-Thérèse gathered the young men before they left the house. "Follow me. It's exceptionally dark tonight. I'll go first. Once we're in the field, hold tight to my hand. The rest of you form a line and hold onto the next person. Do not let go of one another."

One by one, the six airmen followed her through the back door, down the steps, and across the garden. Marie-Thérèse scaled the wall like a rock climber, then waited until each man was over. Lining them up silently to verify they were ready, she led them cautiously out into the fields. They had only gone a short way when they heard a neighbor's dog bark. Immediately, Marie-Thérèse pushed her charges into the ditch and jumped in beside them. "Don't move," she whispered.

The aviators lay in the ditch. Ice broke under their weight exposing a rivulet that seeped into their pants, jackets, socks and shoes. They shivered so violently, one of the airmen imagined the dog could hear the chattering of their teeth.

Finally, the dog stopped barking. Wet and shuddering, the men climbed out of the ditch, joined hands again and continued slowly across the fields. Up and over hedgerows they went—the most difficult part of the terrain—and on to the main north-south route. Marie-Thérèse stopped to check that no patrols were in view, then crossed to the path that led to the *Maison d'Alphonse*. They arrived at the cottage, their feet freezing and sore from walking two miles in sopping socks and shoes.

Jean Gicquel herded Marie-Thérèse's group upstairs. Eleven other airmen were already crouched on the floor waiting for Dumais' instructions. The attic was all but dark. One dim electric light bulb hung from a cord in the center of the ceiling. One man—the Belgian, Harmel—was handcuffed and kept his eyes down. Lee Gordon recognized one of his Paris "roommates," Staff Sergeant Mike Olynik, among the others, but he kept quiet. The look from Dumais warned him to keep his mouth shut.

Dumais introduced himself, as before, as "Captain Harrison," and began his usual instructions. "Hand over your IDs and your dog-tags, any money you're carrying, any papers, or photographs." He explained the route and warned of the descent of the cliff, but his manner was particularly brusque. For the second time, he had been handed responsibility for someone he didn't trust. Gordon had already been vetted, but Harmel was a liability. He would remain in handcuffs but Dumais couldn't let him out of his sight. He pointed out the Belgian to the group and warned them not to speak to him.

Finishing his lecture, Dumais told the aviators to follow him downstairs. "No talking from now on. When you're outside, line up on the path outside the cottage. Stay in a straight line, your hand on the shoulder of the person in front of you. Do not veer more than twelve inches to the left or right. And remember what I said. If you make any sound, one of us takes you back to the house and you get a bullet in your head."

As with the first operation, they were joined at the last moment by two young Breton Resistance agents who had been scheduled by MI-9 to leave that night. Both men would join De Gaulle's Free French Forces (FFL) upon reaching London. The number of evacuees now totaled nineteen.

The line set out, Dumais in the lead with Harmel. Marie-Thérèse, Job Mainguy and Tarzan (Huet)—who would be stationed at the bottom, middle and top of the cliff to signal to the MGB—were placed throughout the line. Le Cornec brought up the rear.

As Lee Gordon maneuvered the path, holding tight to Olynik's shoulder he wondered where in Brittany they actually were. None of the guides had given any inkling of their location. Although Gordon had become used to walking at night over the past year, it seemed to him that this was the blackest of all, and colder than his worst night in Germany. The path was bumpy, the brambles scratched his cheeks, low tree branches scraped the top of his head. He wished he could see the terrain. He worried about descending the cliff in utter darkness. This was different from finding his way through German towns, and there was no way to tell when a Nazi might spring out of the brush. But the thought of reaching England buoyed his spirits.

Forty minutes later, one by one, the aviators began their descent. "Lie on your back—spread eagle. Dig in your heels. If you hear rocks falling from above, cover your head immediately," Gordon repeated to himself as he slid to the cobbles below. He wondered if Harmel was still in handcuffs.

When all nineteen men had made their descent, they crouched in the cave above the beach. Halfway up, Job Mainguy was already sending his Morse code signal to the MGB. Dumais slid down the cliff with Harmel "in tow," handcuffs removed for the descent. Upon reaching the cave, Dumais pushed the Belgian against the wall and re-handcuffed him. Chastened by Dumais' threats, Harmel remained silent.

An hour later, Dumais heard the gentle sound of the surfboats reaching the sand; for this second operation there were four. Dumais led the aviators to the water, exchanged passwords (*"Dinan/Saint Brieuc"*) with Windham-Wright, waited till the sailors had unloaded the heavy suitcases, and then shook hands with each man. Whispers of "Good luck!" and "*Merci!*" were exchanged as the evacuees climbed into the boats.

The boats slipped away from the beach and headed back to MGB 503. The time was around 3:00 a.m. Dumais and his five French colleagues surveyed their cargo. This time there were eight suitcases, all of them heavy—too much of a load to be carried up the cliff. They would have to be taken the long way, via the gully. Fortunately the tide was low enough for this route to be accessible.

An hour later the party arrived at the *Maison d'Alphonse*, where Jean Gicquel was waiting for them. "You took so long," he said to Le Cornec and Dumais, "I thought something had gone wrong."

Dumais grunted. "We had a lot to carry."

As before, several of the suitcases contained arms and money. Others were packed with clothing and shoes. Seven of the cases were destined for Paris. One was for the Shelburne group and included bottles of whiskey, English cigarettes and chocolates. Dumais and his companions shared one of the bottles, then the guides dispersed and headed to their respective homes and accommodations. Dumais left to join Labrosse at the home of the Le Saux family, who provided yet another of Plouha's "safe" houses. Several hours later they received the message that MGB 503 had reached the shores of England.

Opération Bonaparte II had been a success. Now they could sleep!

CHAPTER 6

OPÉRATIONS BONAPARTE III, IV, V
MARCH 16-17; MARCH 19-20;
MARCH 23-24

March 1944 saw substantial Allied advances in North Africa and Italy, continued heavy bombing of Germany and the first bombings of Vienna, Austria. On the Eastern Front, Soviet troops had pushed the Germans further west. In France, the Germans enlarged and extended the forbidden coastal zone in anticipation of an eventual Allied invasion. The Vichy government demanded accordingly that all inhabitants over 65 leave the zone—an order that created panic and fear among the older people. *Where would they go? How could they leave their loved ones? How could they find lodging and food in unknown territory?* Most went into hiding in their own neighborhoods.

Vichy also increased restrictions on the use of electricity and ordered the closing of cinemas, theaters and restaurants. The Germans, for their part, intensified their requisitions of farm machinery, horses and plows. More day laborers were shipped to Germany, leaving farmers in Brittany, in particular, without help to harvest their crops. Appealing to Vichy without success, farmers hoarded whatever produce they could harvest or sold it on the black market.

The Vichy French radio aired continual propaganda, and posters appeared on walls everywhere reminding the French that anyone participating in *terroriste* or anti-Nazi activity would be "tried" and convicted of a capital offense. All trials were carried out by either military or kangaroo courts. Crackdowns against the Underground did not, however, decrease its operations. Resistance members continued to blow up rail lines, as instructed by London. They also cut telephone lines and broke into businesses and homes of suspected Vichy sympathizers to steal typewriters, handguns, money, food, liquor, tobacco and ration coupons.

Those who listened to the clandestine BBC broadcasts at night suspected that the Allies would soon commence their long-awaited European invasion, though the questions of when and where it would occur still remained a matter of much speculation. Churchill had alluded to the likely event in a broadcast on March 26, 1944: "The hour of our greatest effort is approaching ... And when the signal is given, the whole circle of avenging nations will hurl themselves upon the foe and batter out the life of the cruelest tyranny which has ever sought to bar the progress of mankind."

An editorial in a March issue of *Moniteur des Côtes-du-Nord*, a collaborationist newspaper, admonished the French populace that if the invasion indeed occurred, *it is the duty of the* [Vichy] *government to anticipate the worst, for...* [an Allied invasion] *will cause great damage to our country* .

...our soil risks again becoming a battleground, [and] *when destruction follows destruction, is it the moment for the French people to rise up against one another; to hate each other and to kill one another? ... the duty of the French people is to back* [its] *government and obey its orders ...*

In the meantime, as Dumais described it, "the sky was full of Allied planes every night, and bailed-out airmen were dropping all over the north of France." In Paris, Paul Campinchi had as many as 75 men in hiding and constantly faced the difficulty of feeding and clothing them all. Dumais' stated intention was to evacuate "every airman that came down in France," for as long as the Shelburne Line remained a secret to the Gestapo. Even rushing the men straight through Paris to Brittany did little to assist Campinchi, however, as newly downed fliers were arriving from the north faster than Campinchi could empty his safe houses.

Dumais decided to crank up the evacuation process. The first two Bonaparte operations had been planned a month ahead of time, but Dumais figured that MGB 503 could do a cross-channel run every couple of days, provided everything was ready in Plouha. He had Labrosse send a message to London asking MI-9 to schedule not just one but three Bonaparte operations for March—on the 15th, 19th and 23rd—three evacuations in nine days. London asked for confirmation, which Dumais duly sent. Though obsessed with security, Dumais gave Campinchi and Le Cornec the BBC message codes, so they could act directly to ship their "packages" by rail from Paris to Brittany. It helped that Guingamp, which served as the Breton railhead for the Shelburne operation, was outside the coastal exclusion zone, so the arriving airmen did not require *Ausweis* permits in addition to their false ID papers. The Resistance leader in Guingamp, Mathurin Branchoux, would receive the men at the station and hide them in safe houses until he received word from Le Cornec. Since the small train to Plouha was out of service, Guingamp garage owner, François Kérambrun, would drive the men the last 15 miles (23km) to Plouha in his truck.

One of the airmen to be evacuated in the first March Bonaparte operation (*Opération Bonaparte III*) was Second Lieutenant Ralph Patton, a B-17 co-pilot who had been in hiding in central Brittany for two months. Patton's plane was just one of over a hundred B17s that took off from their base in England before dawn on January 5, 1944. Their mission that day had been to bomb the airfield at Merignac (now the site of Bordeaux's international airport), an operational training base for German pilots that held at least 60 fighter planes.

Patton recalled in his memoir, *Flying on a Wing and a Prayer*, that his plane was hit by flak just after they dropped their bombs. The damage wasn't catastrophic, but they were attacked soon after by German Messerschmitt fighters and shot through the tail rudder. Then again, a third time, they were hit by anti-aircraft batteries near Lorient—site of one of the five German submarine bases on the Atlantic Coast.[1] The B-17's pilot, Lieutenant Glenn Johnson, yelled to his crew: "Bailout! Bailout!" Patton recalled that when he reached the escape hatch he saw that the bombardier and navigator had already jumped. *I followed, head first, guessing my altitude to be about 12,000 feet. The plane's slipstream disoriented me, and I held off pulling the D-ring to open the chute for what*

---

1 North to south, the five major bases (with submarine pens) were located at Brest, Lorient, Saint Nazaire, La Rochelle and Bordeaux.

seemed like an eternity. When I finally pulled it, the nylon canopy opened with a jerk and filled with air. Swinging like a pendulum, I could see I was headed for one of Brittany's famous hedgerows.

My chute collapsed into a tree and I hit the ground with a jolt. Panic gave way to reality. I was alive. I was unhurt. But I was in big trouble. I unbuckled my parachute and harness as quick as I could, stashed them under a bush and headed across the field. Johnson and Jack McGough, our bombardier, came running toward me. Several French farmers in the field stared at us without making a move to help us, so we ran toward the woods a few hundred yards away. After ten minutes of running, crawling and climbing over hedgerows, we found a well-concealed spot and stopped for a rest.

The three airmen knew they were near the center of the Breton Peninsula, and that if they traveled any direction except east they would run into the heavily fortified coastal zones, bristling with German troops. They decided their best course of action was to try heading toward Spain and from there, back to England.

Their escape kit included a mini-compass, and after walking eastward for several hours, the three men ran into a farmer and his young son, who used sign language to ask if the aviators were hungry, and gave them some food and a bottle of wine. Thanking the farmer profusely, the men continued eastward. Six hours after bailing out, they could still see a column of black smoke rising from where their plane had crashed.

They took the risk of approaching the stone cottage of another farmer, who found them beds for the night in a larger house belonging to one of his neighbors. On the way, they passed an elegant mansion belonging to people described by their guide, in whispered tones, as *collaborateurs*— people who would gladly have turned the airmen in to the authorities for the 10,000-franc reward. The three airmen were grateful for what they were offered further along the road: *three beds with straw mattresses and down-filled comforters—simple comfort for our first night in France.*

Patton added, *Although I was tired and aching, sleep came fitfully. Questions raced through my mind. What would become of us? How many miles to reach the Spanish border? We had no identification except our dog tags, very few francs in our escape kits, and we were still in our flight outfits. Would we make it to the border without being caught by the Nazis? ... I finally managed to stop worrying and I fell asleep.*

Early the next day, the three men left, trudging eastward across Breton farmlands and hedgerows, wondering when to turn south. In England, they had been told in MI-9 briefings that Resistance members in Brittany would be helpful to downed aviators. However, they had no idea where to contact such people, nor did they know that an evacuation route—the Shelburne Line—operated along the eastern coast of the Breton peninsula. The three men thought only of making it the 400 miles (640 km) to Spain.

Later that day, crossing a road on a hill overlooking the Nantes-to-Brest Canal, they encountered a schoolteacher who warned them of a German observation tower by the canal, and indicated that he would help them. At the same moment, a French gendarme approached them on bicycle. As Patton described it, the teacher "kept his cool," exchanging a few words with the *gendarme* who, like many Breton officials, was sympathetic to the Allies and "looked the other way" whenever possible.

The Frenchman told us to hide behind a hedgerow immediately and that he would return with some food. True to his word, he reappeared at dusk carrying a huge tureen of pureed vegetable soup, which we devoured with gusto.

Then, under cover of darkness, he escorted them across the canal and found them a haystack where they could sleep for the night. A dog barked at them, and the men were obliged to reveal themselves to its farmer-owner as "Americans." The farmer's response was to bring them a bottle of Calvados. Patton wrote that they each took *a healthy swig of the alcohol, which almost cauterized our throats, but we sure slept soundly that night!*

The school teacher returned before dawn the following morning and indicated that he would take the airmen to a monastery where they could get help. Along the way, two figures ran toward them from a drainage ditch. Patton was sure they were Germans and that he, Johnson and McGough were headed directly for a POW camp. But one of the figures threw his arms around Patton and shouted, "Lieutenant, I thought you were dead." It was the left-waist gunner from their B-17, Isadore Viola, and, with him, Second Lieutenant Norman King, the navigator of another bomber that had been shot down the same day as Patton and his crew.

So now, five young men in flight suits, none of whom knew the French language, were climbing hedgerows and marching down roads in a country occupied by a ruthless enemy and any number of locals who would gladly turn them in for the reward money.

When their school teacher guide had done all he could, he gave the airmen a map to the monastery and hurried off in the opposite direction. If *les Boches* or the Vichy government learned that he had helped Allied aviators, he would be shot.

At the monastery, a priest gave each man civilian clothing, though the pair of shoes given to Viola didn't fit, and he developed painful blisters on his feet that left him struggling to keep up with the others as they climbed hedgerows and sloshed through muddy fields. Eventually they came to a road, where they saw a boy, who dashed off in the opposite direction, and a Frenchman who told them they were "*Stupides, stupides!*" indicating with gestures that they should never follow railroad tracks or canals.

Soon after, they came to a town, Plouray, where they entered a bistro and said the word "American." According to Patton, *the owner locked the door at once and served all five of us dinner and wine. We ate and drank till we were completely oblivious to our desperate situation. The wine made us not even care there was a war on.*

Fortunately, the owner of the cafe had connections to the Resistance. After the men had sobered up a little, he led them out of town to a field and told them to lie down until someone came for them. They napped until after dark, when several men and women approached them. One of the women introduced herself in good English as Toni. "I'm the local schoolteacher," she said. "One of my young students saw you earlier and told me to look for you."

The airmen followed Toni and her friends to a two-story schoolhouse. Patton and McGough were assigned beds in Toni's living quarters. Johnson and Viola were housed with Toni's parents. King was hidden in a nearby house, whose owners were unaware that he was sleeping in their loft at night.

For the next five weeks the airmen lived this way—confined during the day to the upper floor of the school where they could only whisper, where they had a single chamber pot for their toilet, and where—for the entire time—they were unable to bathe. As time passed, they pressed their hosts for information. "When will we be evacuated?" They were given no answers and were asked in return for news of *le débarquement* (the invasion). But the airmen had no information to give either.

By the end of February, Toni was finding gifts of wine and rare treats—churned butter, farm-raised chicken, and bread—appearing on her kitchen table. All were items that required many ration coupons or were otherwise impossible to find in the markets. The people who delivered these gifts were Toni's students or friends, but she began to worry. Clearly, too many people knew about the Americans. The mayor of Gourin, a town ten miles (16 kilometers) from Plouray, was head of the local Resistance and had arranged for the airmen to be given false IDs. His people could be trusted, but word could still leak out, particularly among Toni's students. It was time the men were moved. Toni told them that people were working to get them back to England, but they could no longer stay at the schoolhouse. Patton recalled that their good-byes were touching.

Ralph Patton's fake French ID card.

The five men were split up and moved to other villages, other host families. Patton and King spent two weeks in an early-20th-century hotel whose elderly owner had served in the French army in World War I. He hated the Germans and, on occasion, would whip out a large pocketknife, draw the four-inch blade across his throat and utter, *"On les aura, les Boches."* The two aviators had no problem understanding what he meant: "We'll get those dirty bastards."[2]

After two weeks, King and Patton were moved again, this time to an isolated farmhouse where they joined Glenn Johnson and Isadore Viola. McGough's whereabouts were unknown. For another two weeks the four men slept on straw in the attic. They had now been in hiding for over two months. Bored and impatient, they kept asking, "When will we be sent back to England?" Again, their hosts kept reminding them, *"Patience! Patience!"*

Finally, one afternoon, two men pulled up to the farmhouse in a truck. *"Vite, vite! Train, train. En retard! En retard!"* they told the airmen, gesturing urgently. The four Americans understood—they were being taken to a train and would have to hurry. Climbing into the back of the truck they found McGough already crouching inside.

They were driven to the station in Gourin. The two Frenchmen bought the aviators their tickets and told them to get off the train at a place called Guingamp, where they should look for a man carrying a German magazine under his left arm. The five men crammed onto wooden benches in a third class car, squeezed against locals who had been foraging the countryside for eggs, bread and vegetables. They feigned sleep, but at each stop Patton sneaked looks at the German officers patrolling the platforms on horseback.

Fortunately, as Patton wrote, the train arrived late in Guingamp. *The guards had already been withdrawn so we didn't have to show any identification. A man and two girls met us. The man was carrying a newspaper under his left arm—the signal that we were to follow him.*

King, Johnson and Viola were taken to one house. Patton and McGough were taken to another a block from the German headquarters in Guingamp. Against all rules of Resistance activity, Patton's and McGough's landlady, Madame Francine Laurent, kept the names and

---

2 Author's translation.

addresses of all the airmen she helped. She would roll the forbidden piece of paper and insert it into a hiding place in her kitchen stove pipe. Another evader, a Canadian Spitfire pilot, Ken Woodhouse, told of this also, adding that there were thirty-two names on Mme. Laurent's list by the end of the war, and that she also stored arms, ammunition, explosives and radios in her house.[3]

On the airmen's third night in Guingamp, a delivery truck pulled up at the house after dark. Patton recalled, *Two men came in, turned on the radio to the forbidden BBC and listened intently while a series of messages we didn't understand came over the airways. Five minutes later, the driver of the truck got up and said quietly, "Allons-y."* (Let's go.) *He motioned us to climb into the back of the canvas-covered pick-up.*

"What the hell happens if the police stop us?" Patton muttered to McGough.

"We all cook," McGough replied. Toni had told them some of the atrocities committed by the Gestapo, and the men knew it would be the firing squad for all of them, including their driver—François Kérambrun.

Fumes from the *gazogène* engine filled the truck as it rumbled slowly along country roads. It stopped repeatedly along the way to pick up more men, until there were twenty of them crammed together, though Patton and McGough's three fellow B-17 crewmen were not among them. Finally the truck stopped altogether outside a stone cottage and Kérambrun told the men to get out.

The date was March 16 and they had arrived at the *Maison d'Alphonse.*

Inside the cottage, Lucien Dumais greeted this new batch of men in his usual fashion—"I am Captain Harrison of the British Military Intelligence Service"—after which he motioned for Jean Gicquel to lead the group upstairs to the attic. Patton and McGough were pulled aside as their names did not appear on the schedule for evacuation that night. Dumais had no choice but to vet them, then and there. He launched into his usual, intense questioning: "Where do you live in the U.S.? ... What are the

---

3 After the war, in 1954, Ralph Patton returned to Brittany with his wife to look for the people who had helped him evade capture. Mme. Laurent had since passed away—after being awarded the Croix de Guerre, France's highest award for valor—but her nieces had saved all the small pieces of paper, which they showed to the Pattons.

White Sox? ... What's the capital of Illinois? ... Who pitches for the St. Louis Cardinals?" Without hesitation, Patton and McGough spewed out answers. Dumais was satisfied. Both men passed the test.

Upstairs they joined their 18 truck-mates and four other American and British airmen seated on the floor. Dumais gave them his routine briefing. He told the men to turn over their dog tags, their money, anything personal such as photos or letters. Then, as always, he described the path to the cove; how the men should walk holding the shoulder of the person in front; how to maneuver the cliff; and where to hide at the bottom. He ended with the warning that if anyone let out a noise or a sound, they would have their throat slit.

Two unexpected complications increased the danger that night. The first occurred earlier in the day when Job Mainguy and Pierre Huet noticed German recruits planting mines in the fields along the route to the beach. The two Frenchmen went back out before dark, studied the position of each mine—there were seventeen in total—and marked them with white flags attached to sticks.

The second problem had yet to arise.

At midnight, the group set out from the *Maison d'Alphonse*. Each man lined up Indian file, careful not to veer off the path, trying not to sneeze or cough, and nervously following the guides to avoid the mines. They reached the cliff in good time, made their descent safely, then crouched or stood against the overhang at the bottom. The tide was still receding and it would soon be so low the men would have to cross 300 yards (273 m.) of slippery cobbles to reach the water. To Marie-Thérèse Le Calvez, who waited with them, flashlight in hand in case of emergency, it seemed as if the surfboats were taking even longer than usual to arrive.

Suddenly, a round of fire rang out along the coast, reverberating around the cliffs and shaking the ground. The sky lit up like daylight. Baudet, Huet, Le Cornec and Dumais froze, immediately dropped to the ground, each man clutching a Colt .45 that MI-9 had recently sent them from London.

Where was the fire coming from? Pointe de la Tour? Or from the second German battery near Gwin Ségal? Had the Germans detected the MGB?

A few minutes later there was another explosion. Then—nothing.

Silence. Standing against the foot of the rocky cliff, Ralph Patton thought to himself, "My God, we're so close. Don't let us fail now."

Dumais, still at the top, and furnished with a walkie-talkie[4] from the last Bonaparte Operation, radioed the MGB.

Patrick Windham-Wright's voice crackled back. "We're retreating a bit. We can't tell if they're shooting at us. We'll let you know if we can return."

The guides and the airmen waited. An hour passed. There was no further artillery fire. Windham-Wright radioed back to Dumais, "We're moving back in position and lowering the surfboats."

It was late—about 3:00 a.m.—when the men and the guides heard the slapping of oars, and Dumais was able to lead the airmen to the boats.

Ralph Patton was the last to climb aboard. *I breathed easier as the sailor asked if I could pull an oar. You bet I could! We said goodbye as our Resistance team pushed the boats off the beach and headed off to sea, not knowing what to expect. A half-hour of strenuous rowing, and the British sailors homed in on the Motor Gun Boat. We scrambled aboard ... they soon hoisted the rowboats ... and the MGB headed to England. We were homeward bound at last!*

On shore, since the tide was so low, Dumais and the Plouha guides were able to make the long hike up the gully, instead of the cliff, lugging what turned out to be their heaviest haul ever. There were ten cases in all. Most were filled with arms; others contained clothing for future aviators-in-hiding and their hosts. As before, there were also treats for the Shelburne team members.

When they reached the plateau, Huet and Mainguy gathered up the mine marker flags, while the others went ahead to stow the arms in the Gicquels' barn. Each member of the group enjoyed a quick nip of whiskey before they dispersed. They could not afford to linger. Morning was approaching.

Two more *Opérations Bonaparte* (IV and V) had already been scheduled for the nights of March 19-20 and March 23-24. After the artillery scare during the third operation, Dumais that feared that Shelburne had been

---

4 Author's note: The French translation has always amused me: "talkie-walkie."

compromised, so he sent Labrosse ahead to Paris with instructions to radio MI-9 telling them to cancel the next two evacuations. Unknown to Dumais, however, Labrosse had problems with his radio and was unable to make the necessary contact. Dumais followed him to the capital, not realizing that the evacuations were still scheduled to proceed.

Le Cornec now knew the message codes, however, and with the solid support of his team in Plouha he proceeded with plans for the fourth and fifth operations. German security along the coast was increasing every day in anticipation of *le débarquement*. Multiple transfers of airmen from St. Brieuc to Guingamp to Plouha were becoming too risky. Instead, the evacuees would be trucked directly as a group from Guingamp on the evening of each operation. For the Plouha host families this was a relief. Their means of providing for "guests" had run its course—they had exhausted their resources.

Before each of the next two operations, Huet and Mainguy set off to flag the mines, while Le Cornec and the others briefed the airmen in the *Maison d'Alphonse*. Without the bilingual French-Canadian Dumais to give orders, the group relied on sign language and basic *lycée* (secondary school) English. The aviators followed the hand signals without difficulty and the operations went smoothly.

Opération Bonaparte IV, on March 19-20, evacuated eighteen men—17 aviators and one escaped POW. Among this group were the rest of Patton's escape band—pilot First Lieutenant Glenn Johnson, waist-gunner Staff Sergeant Isadore Viola and navigator Second Lieutenant Norman King— and the co-pilot of another B-17, Second Lieutenant Robert Costello.

Opération Bonaparte V, three days later, sent out a total of 28 men— five RAF (including the aforementioned Canadian Spitfire pilot, Ken Woodhouse), 21 USAAF and two young Frenchmen who were being dispatched to London for "missions." One of the Frenchmen, Jean Tréhiou, was a good friend of 18 year-old Marie-Thérèse Le Calvez. On the basis of her abilities, he had originally recommended her to Le Cornec as a potential Shelburne operative.

By the end of this fifth operation, the Shelburne Line had safely evacuated a total of 67 men. Airey Neave was able to report to the US Army Air Force command in London that a "substantial proportion" of airmen had been returned from France within a month of being shot down, and sometimes within just a few days. Neave was not exaggerating. The Canadian Spitfire pilot, Ken Woodhouse, had been on the ground in France a mere eight days.

This was a "miraculous" result, and Neave and his MI-9 colleagues basked in the prestige. The decision had been made, however, that the fifth *Opération Bonaparte* would also be the last. The reasons for this had less to do with the artillery scare of Operation III than the fact that the nights were growing shorter—something Windham-Wright had discussed with Le Cornec on the beach during the fifth operation. MI-9 also knew, however, as the Shelburne operatives did not, that it was essential the Germans not be provoked into strengthening their coastal defenses any further. Toni the schoolteacher and her Resistance friends in Plouray were right: *Le débarquement*—the Allied invasion of France— was coming.

Monument erected above Anse Cochat by the Air Forces Escape and Evasion Society (AFEES). Ralph Patton was one of the founding members of AFEES after the war.

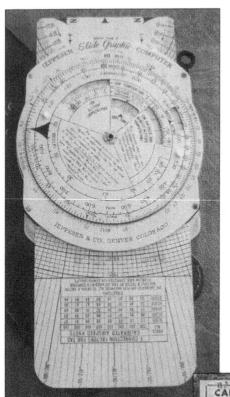

The "Whiz-Wheel" Flight Computer of World War II, used by Second Lieutenant Robert Costello, a B-17 co-pilot who was evacuated in Operation Bonaparte IV

Robert Costello's fake French ID Card

CHAPTER 7

LE DÉBARQUEMENT
(THE INVASION)
JUNE 1944

Beginning June 1, British Intelligence began nightly broadcasts on BBC *Radio Londres*, in French, to Resistance groups around France advising that *le débarquement* (the invasion) was imminent. Coded orders instructed them to blow up bridges and railroad tracks and cut telephone lines of German regional headquarters in Brittany and Normandy. In the background of these broadcasts listeners heard the first four notes of Beethoven's 5th Symphony (dot dot dot dash—'V' for Victory in Morse code). Hindsight suggests this musical snippet was a highly risky inclusion, but it doubtless heartened the Resistance personnel who heard it.

Four days later—on June 5, the night before D-Day—the BBC announced to the French Resistance that *Opération Overlord* was about to begin. The long anticipated coded message was the first stanza of *Chanson d'automne*, a poem by Paul Verlaine, one of France's well-loved poets: *Les sanglots longs /Des violons /De l'automne /Blessent mon coeur /D'une langueur monotone.* (The long sobbing of autumn violins wounds my heart with a wearisome melancholy.) The Resistance, which had long-prepared for this day, sprang into action. That night Vichy Radio reported that more than 1,000 acts of sabotage by *terroristes* had been committed south of the coastline, preventing German reinforcements from reaching the beaches of Normandy.

Although it was well known throughout much of the world by then that an Allied invasion of France was imminent, its exact timing and location remained an extremely closely held secret. Even Allied troops bound for Normandy beaches were not told by senior officers where they were headed until they were on board their transport ships and landing craft. In France, only a handful of local Resistance leaders knew anything of the details, and then only from the radio broadcasts. Lucien Dumais, for example, had guessed the invasion was coming from the type and quantity of stores brought in via the Bonaparte operations, but the first he knew of its actual occurrence was from the BBC announcement on June 6.

The Germans were even more in the dark as to the timing and location of the invasion. So effective were Allied counter-intelligence efforts that many in the German High Command, including Hitler himself, believed the Allies would land in Brittany, somewhere between Cherbourg and Brest. (Plouha lay at the very center of this stretch of coast.) All Atlantic coastal defenses were to be strengthened as a precaution, but General Erwin Rommel, who was assigned this unenviable task, was given too little time and too few resources to carry it out. He had requested six to eight additional Panzer tank divisions, and five to seven motorized divisions as reserves for the Paris area, but his requests remained unfulfilled.

German defensive activities in and around Plouha in anticipation of the invasion took many forms. All business and private telephone traffic was suspended; the placement of mines was extended along the Breton coast, forcing farmers to abandon their fields; and anti-tank trenches were constructed along the old railroad branch line from Guingamp to Plouha. To accomplish the latter, the Germans demanded two days of work per week from all area men between the ages of 18 and 55. Le Cornec, Mainguy, Huet, and the others knew the trenches made no sense strategically, and that the real goal of the Germans was to keep the Breton male population in check.

In other anti-invasion preparations, the Gestapo moved into Army posts in and around Plouha, heightened surveillance activities, and initiated door-to-door interrogations. Every day, at varying hours, German MPs drove a truck around the town with a radio detector installed. Anyone unfortunate enough to be listening to the BBC during these random scans was certain to be arrested and sent to prison.

The cessation of the Bonaparte evacuation operations at least gave the Shelburne members some respite. Nevertheless, they and other local Resistance members remained on edge because of the increased Gestapo, Army and French *Milice* activity. On one occasion, two local *gendarmes*, Garion and Dagorne—clandestine members of the Resistance—warned François Le Cornec that he had been denounced. Le Cornec quickly closed his butcher shop and took to the woods near Guingamp. After hiding out for several weeks, he learned that the accusation had been a false alarm and he returned to Plouha.

In Dumais' absence, and with the cessation of the Bonaparte operations, Le Cornec and other members of the Shelburne Line joined forces with the *Armée Secrète* (A.S., Secret Army), a Resistance outfit led by Marthurin Branchoux in Guingamp. But, from time to time, as Guingamp became overwhelmed with new arrivals of downed Allied airmen, Le Cornec mobilized his colleagues to hide some of them in Plouha.

Once again, Marie-Thérèse Le Calvez and her mother volunteered their house, and by June 1944 they had another seven Allied airmen in residence. Marie-Thérèse recalled that one night around this time, well after curfew, a patrol of the White Russian conscripts from Pointe de la Tour stationed themselves in front of the Le Calvez house. At a pounding on the door, the seven airmen rushed up to the attic to hide.

Marie-Thérèse opened the door. "*Terroristes chez vous?*" one of the Russians asked. ("You have terrorists in your house?") She burst out laughing, "Oh, this village is so small we couldn't possibly hide anything from the Germans."

The Russian looked surprised, but said "*Gut, gut*" ("Good, good") and left to rejoin his group.

Marie-Thérèse was convinced their departure was only an *au revoir* and sure enough, a few days later while she was at her day job as the secretary of the local agricultural cooperative, a villager showed up at the Le Calvez house in a hurry to warn her mother that a German patrol was on its way.

Madame Le Calvez had barely got the airmen out the back door, over the wall behind the house, and into some bushes before the Germans arrived. The airmen remained in place for more than two hours as the

Germans, for reasons unknown, decided to practice their goose-step formation in front of the Le Calvez house.

In mid-afternoon, Marie-Thérèse left work to check on her mother. Trying not to draw attention to herself, but terrified for her mother and the possibility that the Germans would discover their "guests," she ran toward the house. As she did so, one of the goose-stepping German soldiers left the line and hurried into the bushes along the escape path behind her house.

"I was panicked," Marie-Thérèse wrote, "because that was the only possible hiding place for the men in daylight. I followed a short distance behind him. But he stopped short of the house and it turned out he was just *watering the bushes*."

After dark, Marie-Thérèse led the seven aviators back to the house, all of them worried and hungry. "We wanted to laugh about this episode, but our hearts weren't in it. The permanent menace floating in the air became heavier each day," she said.

Another member of Le Cornec's Shelburne team, Georges Ropers, lived with his family in the hamlet of Camblach, north of Plouha. The house was of typical Breton architecture—two-story, with an exterior of variegated brown stones and a steep roof of dark gray slate. Well-suited to aspects of the Shelburne Line's operations in a number of ways, like many other houses in the area, it had a substantial *cave* (cellar) for storing wine. Tall hedges shielded the front of the house from prying eyes on the road between St. Brieuc and Paimpol, while the back door faced a dirt road that led to the *Maison d'Alphonse*, a half-mile away.

Since the advent of the Shelburne operations, the Ropers' cellar had been used to cache weapons. With the recent increase in surveillance and searches along the coast, however, Mainguy, Huet and Gicquel decided that both the *Maison Ropers* and the *Maison d'Alphonse* were too close to the beach and Pointe de la Tour to be used safely any longer. Their concern was heightened by the fact that the Russian conscripts based on Pointe de la Tour—a motley assortment of White Russian thieves, felons, and drunkards—had become even more aggressive than the Germans. In the area surrounding their pillboxes—*Maison d'Alphonse*, Keruzeau and Saint Samson—the Russians saw *terroristes* everywhere. They opened fire

The Ropers' house, Camblach, 2012.

at the slightest provocation and beat on villagers' doors at all times of the night demanding liquor. As yet, not one member of the Shelburne team or the safe house families had been arrested. However, given the situation with the Russians, and fearing a major search by the Gestapo, Le Cornec's team decided it was time to move the weapons and ammunition stored at Ropers' house and the *Maison d'Alphonse.*

On a Monday afternoon when most businesses were closed, Ropers and Huet drew up at the Gicquel cottage with a horse and cart. Hidden among four giant baskets of potatoes was Ropers' cellar "stock." Ropers and Huet had spent the better part of the previous night transferring the heavy weapons and ammunition from his cellar to the cart. At Gicquel's barn, they loaded most of the ammunition, topping their goods with a thick layer of clover and grass. Later that afternoon, they headed to Le Cornec's butcher shop near the town square to unload the weapons, passing within 300 yards of the Nazi headquarters. That day no curious eyes stopped to watch, no one queued up for potatoes, and the men returned to their houses, relieved to have succeeded thus far with the transfer. Later that week, they would move those weapons to Guingamp using Kérambrun's truck.

Over the preceding months, Le Cornec had also relied on the Ropers family to house aviators. This was a particularly risky business for the family since their eldest daughter, Anne, ran a sewing operation on the main floor of the house with two young female apprentices under her tutelage. Five days a week, for nine hours a day, Anne Ropers continued her daily sewing operation without letting on that, up in the attic, a pair of young Allied airmen, suffocating with boredom but sworn to silence, were in hiding, waiting for evacuation to England. A month had passed since the Ropers family had hosted those two visitors, but soon, again, Le Cornec would impose on them once more.

On the night of June 17, 1944—11 days after the first Allied landings in Normandy—Anne's father, George Ropers, heard a knock at the back door. It was midnight, three hours after curfew.

"*Mon Dieu,*" he thought. "This is it—Germans." Le Cornec had warned him that the Gestapo had been in the neighborhood, interrogating and intimidating residents.

Ropers waited a moment. The knock came again. "No . . ." he thought, "This knock has a familiar pattern."

He opened the small window encased in the door, peered out and saw Job Mainguy. Ropers unlocked the door and let in his friend.

"I have some news," Mainguy said.

"In the *cave,*" Ropers said, indicating the way to the cellar.

Downstairs, Mainguy launched into his story: "This morning, when Huet was out checking where the *Boches* had been laying new mines, he spotted three men in the fields. One speaks French; the other two don't. Apparently they've been sleeping in the weeds for a couple of days. Huet said they looked pretty dirty and they're hungry." Mainguy added that the French-speaker had told Huet he and his companions were British and they wanted to get in touch with the Resistance. "But they could be spies, you know. We need to check them out."

Ropers was aware that, two days before, three other men had pounded on Huet's door in the middle of the night. Certain it was the Gestapo, and that this was the end of Shelburne, Huet had opened the door.

But there on his stone doorstep was Jean Tréhiou—Marie-Thérèse Le Calvez's friend—with two companions. Huet couldn't believe his eyes. "What the hell are you doing here, and how did you get here? You walked straight through the minefield!"

Only two months earlier, Tréhiou had left with a group of Shelburne evacuees to undergo commando training in London. This had entailed weeks of classes and practice at "Patriotic School" run by the Free French, and included intensive training in jujitsu, parachuting, mine laying, practicing with arms and explosives, decoding of messages—all critical techniques used in undercover work. Tréhiou's "supreme test" had been similar to the one Lucien Dumais had undergone in 1943. He was parachuted into the country north of London without an ID and furnished with a simple escape kit. For four days he was expected to evade a group of English Home Guard and return safely to London. He accomplished this without difficulty, prompting London to choose him as leader of a new mission: to set up a base in Nord-Finistère, the northwestern section of Brittany from where he and his group were to conduct sabotage operations against the Germans, gather military intelligence, and assist in the recovery of downed Allied airmen.

Tréhiou explained to Huet that he and his two companions had been brought over from Dartmouth by MGB 503 and dropped off on Plage Bonaparte earlier that night. He assumed that the officer and the two sailors who had dropped them off by surfboat had returned safely to England.

British Intelligence knew the entire coastal area had been mined, but nevertheless decided to drop the three French agents there. If any of them had been killed or injured by an exploding mine, the Germans would quickly have realized that Plage Bonaparte was being used as a point of evacuation and entry for the Resistance. Although the Bonaparte evacuations had been halted, it would have meant a final end to all Shelburne Line operations.

From the beach, the three young Frenchmen had come through terrain Tréhiou knew well but without being aware the fields had been mined in his absence. "We had to cut a lot of barbed wire," he told Huet, "but we didn't see any mines. I reconnected the wire before we came here."

Tréhiou and his two companions had since left for Nord-Finistère, but Mainguy and Ropers were still faced with the problem of the three new "British" men out in the fields. After some discussion, they decided to contact "Léon" (Dumais) and ask if he would agree to send Marie-

Thérèse as an intermediary. As Ropers observed, "It's safer to send a girl than a man."

Dumais and Labrosse, who had been undercover in Paris since the last Shelburne operation, had recently returned to the Plouha area. Three weeks after D-Day they had received a message from MI-9 ordering them back to Brittany. The message—"Get to Brittany and stay there!"—meant that the Allies planned to cut off the Breton peninsula, and that MI-9 would have more work for the Shelburne Line as a consequence. The two men traveled by train and bicycle and installed themselves in the attic of the Le Saux-Baudet home in the hamlet of St. Barthélémy, three miles south of Plouha.

Guiguite Le Saux was a friend of Marie-Thérèse Le Calvez, which gave Marie-Thérèse the pretext to cycle to St. Barthélémy on the morning following Mainguy's and Ropers' conversation about the three professed Englishmen. She found Le Cornec, Dumais and Labrosse together in the Le Saux house in the midst of an argument. Dumais had heard some of the locals talking about three men making their way south of town through farming fields near Kernescop, two miles to the north, between Plouha and the coast. He was positive the three men were Gestapo agents and that Shelburne and Plouha were "fried."

"Supposing they really are English," Marie-Thérèse said. "Are we going to let them get picked up under our nose?" Without waiting for an answer, she added, "I know the farmer at Kernescop. Just let me go and walk around."

Neither Labrosse nor Dumais was familiar with Kernescop, and Marie-Thérèse knew that Le Cornec was being watched and didn't want to show his face around town.

"I'll take full responsibility," she told them. Reluctantly, the three men agreed.

The next afternoon, Marie-Thérèse told her mother where she was going, hopped back on her bicycle and took off for the hamlet of Kernescop.

At nineteen, this young woman could invent stories and situations on the spot, and today was no exception. Letting the air out of her tires, she entered the farm and asked her friend to blow them up.

"What are you doing around here?" he wanted to know.

"Oh, I just came by to pick up some flour at your neighbor's mill but both my tires went flat . . ." Then, nonchalantly, she added, "By the way, do you know that everyone's talking about three Englishmen who are supposed to be wandering around here?" When the farmer didn't flinch, she added, "You know it doesn't interest me so much, but my brother is in England and we haven't had any news. If these guys really are English I might be able get some word for Mama."

She had touched a nerve. The farmer had been a friend of her brother. Lowering his voice to a whisper, he told her that, yes, he had hidden the men in a bomb crater in the woods. He offered to take her there.

At the crater site, Marie-Thérèse found the men hunched over in the hole. "We hear you want help," she said, jumping down to land beside them.

"*Bravo, Madame,*" came the reply from one of the men, in French without an accent. He launched into their story. The three of them had come from Dartmouth on MGB 503 to drop off the three French agents. Afterwards, the fog on the water was so thick they had lost their way back in the surfboat. When they finally got to the spot where the MGB had anchored, it was too late—the gun boat had been forced to leave. They rowed back to shore, landing near Port Moguer, a mile southeast of *Plage Bonaparte.*

"We loaded the surfboat with stones, sank it, then stashed our arms and oars in a grotto above the high tide line. We were exhausted by that time so we lay down in the field above the beach and fell asleep. The man who brought you here found us in the morning."

Marie-Thérèse became suspicious. How could they have crossed the fields without setting off the mines? Why hadn't London warned Le Cornec about the arrival of the three French agents? Had they really slept above the beach? There were many unanswered questions. But their story seemed plausible, so against the rules she told the officer her real name.

He smiled and exclaimed, "I thought so. You're quite well known in Dartmouth!"

Marie-Thérèse was stunned by the compliment. That meant the evacuee airmen had talked about staying at her home and they knew her name. "Léon" (Dumais) would not be happy. She thanked the man and said she'd come back for them at 3:00 a.m. the following morning.

Returning home she told her mother to prepare for three more men. As she later wrote, "Mama agreed, as usual, but I could tell she was worried about me and this time she let it show. I tried to joke that this would give us a change from the airmen we'd housed for the past six months. Now we would have some British sailors . . ."

At 2:00 a.m. Marie-Thérèse slipped out the back door and over the wall, praying that no sentry would be stationed behind the German post. The full moon forced her to take a lengthy and circuitous route to avoid being seen. As she crossed the fields toward Kernescop, the pale light revealed a wagon of Russians returning to Pointe de la Tour. They were singing as they went and, as much as she hated to admit it, she found their songs beautiful.

Precisely at 3:00 a.m., Marie-Thérèse arrived at the Kernescop woods. She leaned over the edge of the bomb crater and whispered *"C'est moi."* ("It's me.") The three sailors scrambled out of their hole and stretched their arms and legs. After three nights cramped down out of sight, they were happy to unwind and stand up.

The French speaker introduced himself as Lieutenant Guy Hamilton and the two others as Seamen Dellow and Rockwood. Hamilton was over six feet tall and red-headed. Marie-Thérèse noticed he was also quite handsome.

"You're by yourself?" he asked her, surprised.

"Do you think because I'm a girl I'd be afraid to come by myself?" she replied, annoyed.

Hamilton immediately regretted his question. "I'm sorry," he said. "I didn't mean it that way. Don't worry. I have full confidence in you. All the other airmen think you're marvelous."

"All right then, come. Follow me," she said.

With Marie-Thérèse in the lead, they climbed up and down hedgerows, tripping over ruts, brushing aside prickly bushes, stopping at the slightest noise or the barking of a dog. As they neared the Le Calvez house, they crouched along the path leading to the rear entrance, then heaved themselves over the wall. They had arrived without incident, though their hands and faces were bloodied from brambles.

Upon seeing them, Madame Le Calvez burst into tears. Her daughter was safe. Lieutenant Hamilton, whom Marie-Thérèse called "my tall, red-headed officer," introduced himself to her mother. "My mother was French, my father English," he said, thus explaining his command of the language. The young Seamen, Dellow and Rockwood, who spoke only English, were quite shy.

Each man quickly downed a large bowl of cabbage soup, and Marie-Thérèse led them upstairs. They were filthy but too tired to care. Happy to have had something to eat, they fell asleep at once.

Marie-Thérèse slept at her usual guard post on the floor by the front door. At dawn, after just two hours of sleep, she hopped on her bike again and rode to St. Barthélémy, where Dumais and Le Cornec had waited anxiously all night for her return.

"I gave them my report," she later wrote, "and for the first time since I became acquainted with Léon (Dumais), I saw intense emotion flash over his face."

With a soft tone in his voice, he said, "Marie-Thérèse, if the sailors had been picked up, even admitting they could have resisted interrogation or torture, their presence alone would have alerted the enemy to the comings and goings along this coast. All would have been lost! You have saved the Shelburne Line."

The next step was to move the three Englishmen farther away. Too many people in Plouha had heard about them and the Le Calvez house was dangerously close to the German Post, which now housed officers of the Gestapo.

Several nights later, when the moon was on the wane, Marie-Thérèse told them, "This is it. Time to move. For safety, I'm taking you out of town." Her plan was to lead them to the Ropers' house.

The walk wasn't easy on the moonless night. "Her" officer, Hamilton, fell into an anti-tank trench and broke his nose. The pain was excruciating, but he ground his teeth together and didn't let out a sound. He arrived at Ropers with his nose swollen, his eye sockets black, his cheeks purple, and for two weeks he looked like he'd been in a brutal boxing match.

During weekdays, Hamilton and the two sailors were obliged to remain in the Ropers' attic. But at times, on the weekend, they were allowed "out." Hamilton, who could pass himself off as a Frenchman and relative of the Ropers, enjoyed the most liberty, but not until his face had regained its normal complexion.

One Saturday, Huet and Mainguy took him to Madame Le Meur's café to play a game of *boules*. Among the group of players were several German officers, and somehow word leaked to Dumais about the outing. Furious, he showed up at the Ropers' back door, threatening to take Hamilton into the woods and shoot him. After a lot of fast talking, Georges Ropers calmed Dumais down and sent him on his way.

On weekends, the Ropers' house swelled with family. Anne's two sisters, who worked in St. Brieuc, rode their hard-rubber-tired bikes the fifteen and a half miles (24 km) to Camblach. Her brother, who worked in Guingamp, returned home also. The four Ropers offspring, Anne's grandmother (a permanent part of the family), the two parents, plus Hamilton and his two sailors added up to a total of ten individuals—only seven of whom had coupons for the paltry food rations allowed each week.

Anne Ropers with American dog-tags, 2012.

Preparing enough food for the family and the three men was thus a major challenge. Anne would rise at 4:00 a.m., ride her bike the five miles (8 km) to Plouha, and line up by 5:00 a.m. in front of the butcher shop, along with other hopeful villagers, to buy the week's meat allowance. This was less than a quarter pound (200 grams) per person, but often, by the time Anne reached the door of the shop, no more meat was available. Fortunately, the Ropers had a walled garden where they grew cabbages, turnips, carrots and potatoes—vegetables many French people could no longer stomach after the War.

One Sunday, Anne and one of her sisters set out early in the morning to gather *fraises du bois*—tiny, sweet strawberries that grow wild in the woods. They filled two wooden baskets and returned home to prepare a special dessert for the main meal of the day. Madame Ropers had managed to save the family's meager monthly portions of flour, butter, and sugar as ingredients for a strawberry tart. Before the end of their dinner, Anne took the full tart-pan up to the attic with a knife so Hamilton, Dellow and Rockwood could each cut a slice for himself. When she returned ten minutes later nothing remained in the 16-inch-diameter pan. The three "guests" had no clue what a sacrifice the seven-member family had made that day.

Dumais, in the meantime, was anxious that Room 900 recommence evacuation operations from *Plage Bonaparte*, as the number of airmen in the area was becoming unmanageable. Some were sent on to Spain—98 of them ultimately made the overland journey—but the beach pick-ups remained the most efficient means of repatriation. MI-9 had yet to send instructions in the aftermath of the D-Day invasion, but Dumais was impatient and talked with his Plouha colleagues about asking London to schedule a new evacuation. German surveillance had increased along the cliff path to Anse Cochat but, at the right tide level, they could use the route through the *goulet* (ravine) to get the airmen to the beach.

Mainguy demurred. "Hell no, it's too dangerous. The coast is all mined now—even along the goulet. Huet and I marked the mines along the path from Gicquel's cottage to the cliff while you were in Paris. But the ravine is a different story. It's rough terrain."

"That doesn't matter," Dumais said. "You need to look for the mines."

"I told you, it's not so easy to do."

Dumais placed himself in front of Mainguy, frowning and speaking through his teeth. "I don't care. Figure it out and do it quickly! Understand?"

Mainguy saw that Dumais was not about to back down, and said he'd ask Huet to help him the next day.

Finding the mines along flat land had been relatively straightforward. But locating the mines along the *goulet* meant searching through tall, heavy thickets of prickly gorse bushes. After that the two men would have to figure out how to mark the mines in the undergrowth—all during daylight hours.

In March, MI-9 had sent them a long-handled mine detector, which Huet and Mainguy used to search the *goulet* for the next two days. They discovered 17 more mines and, at the high point, two 203mm shells. Both the mines and the shells were attached by wire to a wooden springboard that would set off the explosives if someone stepped on the board. The springboards were concealed under big clumps of earth among the gorse. Anyone who set off a mine would be blown to bits, and the entire population of Plouha would be accused of collaborating with the enemy.

Mainguy thought about news he had read recently in a leaflet circulated by the Underground press. Just a few weeks before, on June 10, the SS had massacred the entire population of a small village in the center of France. In retribution for killing one of their officers, the SS had rounded up all the men of Oradour-sur-Glane, shot them all, then herded the women and children into a church and set fire to the building. The whole village—more than 642 people—had been murdered.[1] "The Nazis are butchers," Mainguy thought. "That's what will happen to Plouha if Huet and I fail this assignment." He felt sick to his stomach.

The two men pushed on, one keeping watch while the other worked. As they had along the *Chemin Shelburne*, they carefully measured the distance between each mine and drew a diagram showing the position. They hammered a yard-long stick into the ground at each point so they could attach white flags before an evacuation.

At the end of the second day, with their work completed, they returned home, their faces and hands severely scratched, their eyes itching and swollen from pollen of the flowering gorse.[2] But the mines were marked. The Shelburne Line was ready to resume operations. All they needed was the word from London.

---

1 The Nazi general responsible for this massacre was caught and executed by the FFI in September 1944.
2 One spring in the course of doing research for this book, Don and I walked the nearby *Chemin des Douaniers* (old Customs officers' path). It was early May and the path had not yet been weeded. The gorse, akin to Scotch Broom, was tall and in full bloom. Ivy, vine maple, juniper and grasses wove their branches through the gorse. Our jackets were covered with yellow pollen and dirt, and our eyes itched. By the time we exited the path two miles on, our eyes were swollen into slits. We sympathized mightily with Huet and Mainguy that day and from then on!

CHAPTER 8

OPÉRATIONS CROZIER I, II AND III
JULY · AUGUST 1944

While Dumais, his colleagues and their "guests" waited in Plouha, and the Allied advance continued towards Paris, German V-1 guided missiles, known as "buzz bombs", were causing horrendous devastation in London. Launched from missile sites near Calais, these attacks began on June 13, 1944, a week after D-Day, and caused some 30,000 casualties until they finally ceased four months later. London continued to function, nevertheless, as it had done during the Blitz in 1940-41, and Airey Neave, in Room 900 of the British War Office, set about planning a new evacuation operation from Anse Cochat. Neave felt that the code name *Opération Bonaparte* was past its secure "use by" date. Therefore, any new operations would be assigned the name *Crozier*. The radio code phrases were changed also:

Louis Philippe fut un bon roi. (Louis Philippe was a good king) meant "Wait."

La classe salue bien les amis. (The class greets its friends well) meant "Evacuation to take place."

Les vins vieux sont les meilleurs. (Old wines are the best) meant "Operation cancelled."

During the early part of July, only the "*Louis Philippe…*" message was broadcast, as heavy northeast winds and exceptionally rough seas off the coast of Brittany prevented any possibility of an evacuation operation being scheduled.

In the meantime, the atmosphere in and around Plouha was increasingly laden with fear. Around 2:00 a.m. on June 30, Job Mainguy, whose house stood near the center of the village, was awakened by the sound of a Citroën a few feet from his front gate. Three Germans got out and began arguing in the middle of the street. Finally they went into the hotel across the street and the car took off. Two hours later it returned and picked up the three men. Was the Gestapo having a meeting? Or were the agents "visiting" *les prostituées?*

Around 10:00 a.m., the Citroën returned. This time it dropped off four men, one with a german shepherd on a leash. Up one side of the street and down the other, the dog sniffed at each door. This was the Gestapo in action, and for Mainguy it was too close for comfort. No knock came on his door, but as soon as the Citroën departed he packed up his wife and children and took them to his mother-in-law's house at Dernier Sou, a hamlet on the north side of Plouha a short distance from the Ropers' house. Several days later, on the evening of July 5, Mainguy was on his way to Dernier Sou to check on his family when a Russian patrol followed, then stopped him. Surrounding the house, one of the men forced open the front door and shouted at Mainguy's two young children. Mainguy was later to write:

They struck the ground with the stock of their rifles and called me a terroriste. *I couldn't move, and my kids were howling with fear in the kitchen. One of the Russians went in and slapped my five-year-old daughter. For half an hour, this game went on and I wondered how it was going to end, when a German patrol came by on bicycles, heading toward Plouha. The Russians motioned them to the house and soon we had six Germans and five Russians inside.*

I thought we were lost, but somehow I kept my cool. One of the Germans was standing against the cellar door where I had hidden my pistol, my submachine gun and my mine detector. Thank God they didn't open the door and go down to search. Both patrols spoke German and I heard the word terroristes *pronounced many times. But the Germans treated us decently. Their chief, who spoke good French, asked for my papers. With his machine gun at my back, he followed me into the bedroom, rifled through my papers and found my* carte de sécouriste *[first aid card] that showed I was a member of the Passive Défense of Plouha. He turned my card over several times, flipped it back and forth, as if trying to determine its validity. He paused for a moment, then looked straight at me and said, "That's all right, Monsieur. You're not a terroriste."*

He told the Russians to get the hell out, shook my hand and said once more. "It's all right, Monsieur."

I owe my life to that card and to that German. Otherwise, my family and I would have been hauled off and shot within minutes.

Mainguy remained overnight with his family at Dernier Sou. But again, the following night, an hour after midnight, he heard a loud ruckus. A Russian patrol—perhaps the same rowdy group from the night before—entered the courtyard and started shooting off ammunition in every direction.

"On the floor, no lights, don't move," Mainguy told his family. For half an hour they lay on the floor, not daring to move. Mainguy was sure the soldiers had returned for him, ignoring the German officer's reprieve. But, despite the shouting and shooting, the Russians did not try to break in and eventually they departed. The children were terrified and whimpered softly, and none of the family slept the rest of the night. In the morning, they found thirty-five spent cartridges lying in the courtyard.

Up to this time, the other members of the Shelburne Line had been carrying out their regular, non-evacuation activities—retrieving weapons and equipment dropped by parachute for the *Armée Secrète* near Guingamp, and locating food for the men lodged at the Ropers' and Gicquels'. Everything had gone well to date. But their margin of safety was decreasing significantly. On July 7, four Gestapo agents made an unannounced call on the Plouha *gendarmerie*. They declared they had evidence that an escape line was functioning in the area. They knew the names of the individuals, they said, but gave no particulars.

Gendarmes Garion and Dagorne waited till the four agents had left, then set off at once to warn Le Cornec, Huet, and Mainguy. The consensus of Dagorne and the others was that, if the Gestapo had truly known names, they would not have bothered going to the police station, they would have made arrests immediately. This incident was proof, nevertheless, that Plouha was under serious surveillance and Shelburne could be easily compromised. Clearly, it was critical to move the men waiting for evacuation—at that time, ten *chez* Gicquels, five *chez* Le Calvez, and the three English sailors *chez* Ropers. Each family quickly moved out its lodgers. Fortunately, since it was summertime, for the next few days the men slept in either a wheat field or an abandoned barn, with their families sneaking food to them whenever they could.

The Germans remained suspicious that something was going on in Plouha. That same week they installed a radar tower between the town center and the coast. However, this tower had a fixed antenna, meaning it was focused in one direction only. (With a movable antenna the comings and goings around the *Maison d'Alphonse* and the position of the MGB, when it eventually arrived, would certainly have been detected.) At the same time, the Germans and Russians had taken to marching on the road past the *Maison d'Alphonse*. Afraid that the enemy would discover that the mines had been marked with sticks, Huet and Mainguy stood daily watches along the *Chemin Shelburne*.

With the entire coast now in a constant state of alert, the Germans increased their routine patrols in the area. Fishermen were prevented from leaving port. Nightly firings from the gun emplacements occurred more frequently. And night after night came the message for the Shelburne operatives from London: *"Louis Philippe..."* Wait.

Finally, on the evening of July 12, when Labrosse tuned to the BBC, the long-awaited *"La classe salue bien ses amis!"* was among the messages. Dumais organized the collection of the evacuees, while Huet and Mainguy rushed out to place the white rags on the mine marker-posts. The sky was clear but moonless and the two men had trouble locating the posts in the dark. They were on the verge of giving up when Mainguy noticed a glow-worm just a few feet from where he was standing. The worm had attached itself to a tall fern next to the mine.

"Call it what you want," Mainguy wrote, "but for us that worm was a miracle—he directed us to the mine! We couldn't have tried leading the group down this path otherwise. It would have been too dangerous."

Mainguy and Huet completed their task, but as they exited the ravine a German patrol arrived. The two Frenchmen took to the ground, flattening themselves behind an embankment. Mainguy whispered to Huet, *"Ça va mal ce soir."* ("Things aren't going so well tonight.") The patrol finally passed and the two made it back to the *Maison d'Alphonse* where Dumais was in the process of briefing the evacuees, explaining the procedures to take as they descended to the beach.

"Tarzan (Huet) and Job (Mainguy) will lead," he told them. "They know where the mines are. When they approach a mine they will whisper, '*Attention! Mine.*' Each person is to pass the word in the same way."

There were thirteen evacuees in the group—four USAAF and six RAF airmen, plus the three British sailors (Hamilton, Dellow and Rockwood) from the Ropers house. They and their guides left the cottage in single file. Marie-Thérèse and Francis Baudet brought up the middle of the line, Dumais and Le Cornec the tail end. They arrived at the ravine without incident, but when they reached the bottom the sky suddenly lit up. Loud explosions emanated from the north, one after another. Huet stopped in his tracks. Everyone froze, waiting, not knowing what to expect. Were the guns firing at the MGB? Eventually the message was passed along: "Keep moving." Down in the cove the tide was high. The men slogged through knee-high water to reach the cave at the foot of the cliff, then stood with water lapping at their feet.

Mainguy scrambled uphill to his usual position and began signaling with his blue flashlight. Marie-Thérèse remained at the cave with her red flashlight mounted inside a tube to direct the light straight to the MGB. Sometime after 1:00 a.m. the firing ceased, but Mainguy kept signaling for another hour.

At that point, Dumais told the group to be prepared to return to the *Maison d'Alphonse*. It appeared that the MGB had taken off. But then, three minutes later, at 2:25 a.m., they heard the sound of oars, and three surfboats pulled up onto the cobbles near the cave. The usual passwords— "*Dinan/Saint-Brieuc*"—were exchanged between Dumais and Windham-Wright. Three heavy black canvas-covered suitcases were unloaded. After a few quick good-byes, the men climbed one by one into the surfboats.

Lieutenant Hamilton was the last to load. As he shook hands with Dumais, he looked at Marie-Thérèse and said, "Marie-Thérèse, I owe my life to you. I will never forget you. What can I do for you?"

"Try to get some news about my brother when you arrive in England," she said. "That will be the greatest gift you can give Mama and me."

He promised he would find out what he could, then embraced her and climbed aboard his boat.[1]

The operation had taken just five minutes. This was just as well, as July 12 was among the shortest nights of the year, with nautical twilight—the time at which the horizon would gradually become visible from the shore—starting at approximately 2:30 a.m., and sunrise would occur a mere hour and three-quarters later. If the firing of the guns from the onshore emplacements had continued any later than it did, the mission would doubtless have been aborted, as the MGB would have become an increasingly visible target.

Ten days later, on July 23, Dumais, Le Cornec and Labrosse brought five new Allied servicemen to the *Maison d'Alphonse* to await evacuation. Two of these men were members of the British Special Air Service (SAS), which operated in France for three weeks in June-July of 1944 to train, arm and unify local Resistance groups and *Maquis* (loosely organized guerilla fighters) after D-Day. Having carried out their mission in Bois de la Salle—a large forest south of Plouha—the SAS officers had been ordered by London to return to England at once. For Dumais and his colleagues, who had also been working with the Bois de la Salle *Maquis*, this meant a second Crozier operation would have to be carried out.

Dumais and Le Cornec left the five men with the Gicquels and proceeded to the Le Calvez house where Labrosse had just set up his radio to await instructions from London. Soon after their departure, Mimi Gicquel heard noises outside the cottage. The five servicemen, ensconced in a small downstairs room, stopped talking at a knock on the door. Thinking that Dumais and Le Cornec had returned, Jean Gicquel opened the door. Two drunken Russians stood on the doorstep. Gicquel slammed the door in their face and yelled, "Go up to the loft, now!" to his "guests".

The two Russians pushed open the door in time to see the last man climb through the trap door to the attic. Hollering "*Terroristes ici, tous kaputt!*" (Terrorists here, everyone done for!), they aimed their guns at the trap door and let forth a series of bullets that penetrated the ceiling

---

1 Hamilton returned several weeks later on MGB 502 as navigator for *Opération Crozier II*. He was the bearer of sad news for Marie-Thérèse and her mother. Her brother, Georges, had disappeared in a mission over Africa in 1941.

and flooring above. Outside, shots rang out in every direction. Then, suddenly, the shooting stopped.

Gicquel was pulled outside, where the two Russians pointed to one of their men who lay on the ground moaning and with blood oozing from his stomach, obviously shot by his own drunken comrades. The lead Russian pointed a gun at Gicquel's back and ordered him to find a cart to carry the wounded man back to their post. Gicquel quickly went to a neighbor's house, borrowed a cart, and returned to let the Russians load their man. The sound of the cart setting off and the voice of their host bidding *bonne nuit* (good night) calmed the five men in the attic somewhat. They were all dressed in civilian clothes. They had no false IDs. If taken, they would have been treated as *terroristes*, turned over to the Gestapo and shot.

Gicquel and his neighbor followed the cart for a while to assure themselves the Russians had all left. Fortunately this group was not based at nearby Pointe de la Tour, but at Lanloup, a village to the northwest of Plouha. Returning to the cottage, Gicquel found Mimi preparing to leave with their six-week-old baby for his mother's house, a half-mile away.

Gicquel herded the five servicemen to a field away from the house, then rushed to the Le Calvez house to give Le Cornec and "Léon" (Dumais) the news.

"We've got to get you out tomorrow with the other men," Dumais told Gicquel. "The neighborhood is 'cooked.' There'll be searches of Saint Samson as soon as it's light. Stay here till we come for you tomorrow night."

Dumais had it right. At dawn the next morning, July 24, Russian and German troops flooded the neighborhood, searching houses and brutally questioning residents. With the occupants of the *Maison d'Alphonse* nowhere to be found, the cottage was pillaged. At 4:00 p.m. explosions rocked the area. The Gicquels, the Mainguys, the Huets, Marie-Thérèse and Madame Le Calvez, the Ropers, the Le Meur Family, and everyone else in Plouha felt the concussions and saw a pillar of smoke rise 300 feet (100 meters) into the air. One of the explosions came from a stash of arms and ammunition that been left in the Gicquel barn since the first Crozier operation, and which the Germans had failed to find until the barn was set alight and the arms exploded. The smoke also indicated the end of the

Maison d'Alphonse. The cottage had been an essential staging post in the six previous Shelburne operations. Now it was a charred pile of rubble.

Opération Crozier II would still take place that night. Dumais and seven guides would accompany the six evacuees. Le Cornec had asked for reinforcements from a half platoon of the *Maquis* at Bois de la Salle. Stationed at the top of the cliff, they would provide back-up with machine guns. Another *maquisard* would wait at a specified hiding place with a horse and cart to haul arms and ammunition brought ashore from the MGB. Each guide, Marie-Thérèse included, and each evacuee would be furnished with a pistol. It was too risky for them to use the ravine—the Germans were patrolling it all the time now. The Crozier group would have to take the original route down the cliff.

At 10:30 p.m., after meeting the five servicemen in the field, Dumais, Gicquel and the others made their along the path. As they crossed the prairie, their movement set dogs barking, followed immediately by bursts of firing. Each time, the group stopped to let the noise subside, and eventually they reached the minefield. There were no German patrols—no one would be foolhardy enough to venture across such a dangerous area on such a dark night. Nor were there any warning flags in place. But Mainguy and Huet, who had marked the mines in late March, had memorized their locations. They took the lead; Marie-Thérèse, Gicquel and two members of the *Maquis* followed; then came Dumais bringing up the rear with the five servicemen. A *Maquis* machine gunner, placed at the top of the cliff with six other lookouts, would remain there until the Plouha guides returned. From that location they could still smell the smoke, see the glow of red cinders and hear shouts coming from the Germans at the *Maison d'Alphonse.* From time to time, bursts of shooting could be heard further inland.

Having crossed the minefield, each member of the outgoing group adopted a spread-eagle position, dropped down the cliff, and made his or her way to the cave. Mainguy remained at his usual position halfway down to begin transmitting Morse code signals to the MGB with his flashlight. Several small boats, obviously German, were circling in the bay, but Mainguy's position was such that they would be unable to see his light.

Around 1:30 a.m., Mainguy heard the swish of oars. Three surfboats pulled up on the sand at the foot of the beach. Windham-Wright hopped out, exchanged passwords with Dumais, and the sailors—armed to the teeth like the evacuees—unloaded fifteen suitcases of weapons and other supplies.

The five servicemen, along with Jean Gicquel, hopped into the surfboats and disappeared into the night. They would reach England safely in seven hours.

As the Shelburne team left the beach they heard planes approaching. Five or six fighter planes flying at low altitude and causing an "infernal noise," circled round and round above the beach for five minutes, then took off.

"At first, we thought they were Jerries," Mainguy later wrote, "but Dumais surmised it was the RAF coming to support the operation. Fortunately, if strangely, there was no reaction from either the Russians on Point de la Tour or the German post at Pointe de Plouha."

Mainguy continued: "Once we reached the minefield and met the lookouts and machine gunner, we had enough personnel to continue carrying the heavy loads across the minefield to the horse and cart. We loaded the guns and ammunition into the cart stuffed with hay and the horse took off with its owner to deliver the 'goods' to the *Maquis* at Bois de la Salle."

A third Crozier operation—and the eighth and final Shelburne evacuation—was carried out on August 8-9, 1944, in the midst of the German retreat from parts of Brittany. Plouha had been liberated by the Allies on August 6, though the Germans continued to hold on to Brest and other Breton ports for several more weeks as the main body of Allied troops made their way towards Paris. The Shelburne operatives continued to carry weapons, as isolated Germans remained in the area, but the guard post at Pointe de al Tour had been abandoned several days before, to everybody's enormous relief.

With the *Maison d'Alphonse* no longer available as a rendezvous point, François Kerambrun delivered the three men who were to be evacuated—one British officer and two French agents—to a fountain near Kerazeau in the early morning of August 9. The Plouha team led them from there through the minefield and on down to Anse Cochat. Job Mainguy recalled that there were "no incidents, no more fear of the guns on Pointe de la Tour"—and for the first time, they could see the British vessel (MGB 718) waiting offshore, her silhouette appearing as the sun rose.

A single surfboat arrived to collect the three men. There were no arms or other goods to go ashore, but the sailors lingered for a few minutes, offering cigarettes and exchanging pleasantries with the Frenchmen. For the first time, everyone's faces could be clearly seen. Mainguy gestured up at the pillboxes on Pointe de la Tour, which were "no longer a worry." Finally, the surfboat departed, with a profusion of warm thanks and good wishes all round. As MGB 718 prepared to weigh anchor, the Shelburne team climbed back up from the beach, re-crossed the minefield and returned to Plouha aboard Kérambrun's waiting truck.

With this third Crozier Operation, the Shelburne evacuations by sea came to an end. As Airey Neave[2] put it: "Thus ended one of the most splendid exploits in which the Navy and agents of Room 900, aided by French patriots in Paris and Brittany, took part." One hundred and twenty-one Allied servicemen men and nine French agents had been safely evacuated from under the very noses of the enemy, without a single life lost in eight separate operations.[3]

Job Mainguy was more circumspect: "We could ask how much time the Line could have held if the war had continued or if the invasion had failed. It was a question of time and circumstances. Without doubt, luck aiding, we could logically have held still more operations because we weren't yet 'cooked,' but we felt that the danger was becoming clear." The truth in this assessment was contained in Gestapo files discovered in Saint Brieuc after the Liberation, which revealed that Mainguy and Huet had already been listed as "*terroristes* in relation with England."

Lucien Dumais, for his part, was relieved that "all in all, we considered ourselves lucky to have escaped without casualties; one house burnt down

---

2 Airey Neave DSO, MBE, MC, TD, became a barrister after the war. In 1974 he was elected as a Conservative Member of the British Parliament and later served as Shadow Secretary of State for Northern Ireland. He was assassinated in 1979 by an IRA car bomb.

3 One eventual casualty was Lt. Michael Marshall, skipper of the MGB 503, who perished with his vessel and all but two of his crew after encountering a rogue mine off the coast of Norway in May 1945, a few days after V-E Day.

was the sole cost."

Although no further sea evacuations were conducted, the Shelburne Line functioned as an escape line through the autumn of 1944. Members of the Plouha team joined forces with the *Maquis du Bois de la Salle* and helped to evacuate a large group of airmen from a tent camp in the Forêt de Freteval, near Le Mans. Dumais and Labrosse both received commissions in the Canadian regular forces at this time. Dumais was promoted to Captain, Labrosse to Lieutenant.

None of the other Shelburne operatives learned the true names of the two French-Canadians until long after the war. They remained "Léon" and "Claude" until finally, at a reunion of evaders and escapees organized twenty years later, in Buffalo, New York, by Ralph Patton (the USAAF Second Lieutenant whose experiences are recounted in Chapter 6 of this book), their real names were revealed for the first time to some of the airmen they had helped. Anne Ropers and her friend Guigitte Le Saux Pierre attended a later reunion and found Dumais to be charming, warm and sociable. This was far removed from the stern, unsmiling "Léon" Anne Ropers had known during the war, but as she observed, "It was thanks to his discipline and severity that Shelburne was so successful!"

This was undoubtedly true, but as Airey Neave acknowledged, the Shelburne Line was a collaborative effort. Lucien Dumais was the on-site leader, but several dozen other people were directly involved, and all played an essential role in the evacuation operations. Most considered the Allied victory over Nazi Germany to be a reward in itself, but following the end of the war all of the Shelburne agents and safe house families were given decorations, citations and medals by the French government, the British, the Canadians and the Americans. In spite of this, the courage, initiative and determination of "ordinary" people like Marie-Thérèse Le Calvez and her mother, the Gicquels, the Ropers family and all the other inhabitants of Plouha mentioned in this story essentially remained, for the longest time, merely one more untold story of the War.

A monument now stands at the site of the former Maison d'Alphonse. *The inscription, loosely translated, reads: "Here stood the Maison d'Alphonse, destroyed 24 July 1944. 135 aviators brought down onto French soil were assembled and briefed here before being taken to Bonaparte beach and turned over to the Royal Navy for repatriation to Great Britain. Eight evacuations took place from January-July 1944. These perilous missions were accomplished in the black of night across mined zones that were strictly watched by the enemy."*

OPÉRATIONS BONAPARTE AND CROZIER EVACUEES
List of Allied Military Personnel

Opération Bonaparte I,	*Opération Bonaparte II,*
28- 29 January 1944	**26-27 February 1944**
Flying Officer S.P.J. Blackwell, RAF	Flt. Sgt. L.J.G. Harmel, RAF
Sgt. N.B. Cufley, RAF	2nd Lt. M.L. Church, USAAF
Sgt. J. Harvey, RAF	2nd Lt. L. Feingold, USAAF
1st Lt. D.J. Heskett, USAAF	2nd Lt. E.H. Hugonnet, USAAF
1st Lt. R.M. Smith, USAAF	2nd Lt. J.A. Schneider, USAAF
2nd Lt. W.H. Booher, USAAF	2nd Lt. W.C. Tarkington, USAAF
2nd Lt. S. Casden, USAAF	Tech. Sgt. K.O. Blye, USAAF
2nd Lt. M.B. Shapiro, USAAF	Tech. Sgt. J.N. Quinn, USAAF
Tech. Sgt. A.F. Hathaway, USAAF	Staff Sgt. L.C. Gordon, USAAF
Tech. Sgt. A.M. Mele, USAAF	Staff Sgt. D.D. McLeod, USAAF
Staff Sgt. W.E. Dickerman, USAAF	Staff Sgt. H.L. Minor, USAAF
Staff Sgt. J. Eshuis, USAAF	Staff Sgt. M. Olynik, USAAF
Staff Sgt. J.A. King, USAAF	Staff Sgt. J.P. Semach, USAAF
Staff Sgt. W. Sentkoski, USAAF	Sgt. H.O. Gilley, USAAF
Sgt. F.T. Schmidt, USAAF	Sgt. M.A. Hall, USAAF
Sgt. J.L. Sullivan, Jr., USAAF	Sgt. R.A. Schwartzburg, USAAF
	Sgt. R.C. Southers, USAAF

Opération Bonaparte III, 16-17 **March 1944**

Sgt. D. Brown, RAF	Tech. Sgt. K.P. Christian, USAAF
2nd Lt. S.D. Berry, USAAF	Tech. Sgt.W.C. Lessig, USAAF
2nd Lt. J.A. Birdwell, USAAF	Tech. Sgt. H.R. Vines, USAAF
2nd Lt. W.T. Campbell, USAAF	Staff Sgt. R.K. Fruth, USAAF
2nd Lt. P.A. Capo, USAAF	Staff Sgt. F.J. Moast, USAAF
2nd Lt. E.J. Donaldson, USAAF	Staff Sgt. R.L. Paquin, USAAF
2nd Lt. J. McGough, USAAF	Staff Sgt. E.E. Stump, USAAF
2nd Lt. R.K. Patton, USAAF	Sgt. C.W. Creggor, USAAF
2nd Lt. M.M. Rogoff, USAAF	Sgt. C.W. Mielke, USAAF
2nd Lt. W.H. Spinning, USAAF	Sgt. N.B. Parker, USAAF
2nd Lt. D.W. Tate, USAAF	Sgt. C.A. Van Selus, USAAF
2nd Lt. C.B. Winkelman, USAAF	
Tech. Sgt. J.A. Amery, USAAF	

Opération Bonaparte IV, 19-20 March 1944

1st Lt. F.P. Hennesy, USAAF
1st Lt. G.G. Johnson, USAAF
1st Lt. E.J. Wolf, Jr., USAAF
2nd Lt. R.L. Costello, USAAF
2nd Lt. N.R. King, USAAF
2nd Lt. R.O. Lorenzi, USAAF
2nd Lt. J.A. McGlynn, USAAF
2nd Lt. P.E. Packer, USAAF
2nd Lt. C.C. Richardson, USAAF
2nd Lt. R.F. Schafer, USAAF
Tech. Sgt. E.D. Risch, USAAF
Staff Sgt. L.F. Bergeron, USAAF
Staff Sgt. Paul F. Dicken, USAAF
Staff Sgt. W.J. Scanlon, USAAF
Staff Sgt. E.J. Sweeney, USAAF
Staff Sgt. I.C. Viola, USAAF
Cook Buland Khan, escaped POW, Royal Indian Army Service Corps

Opération Bonaparte V, 23-24 March 1944

Pilot Officer R.W. Daniel, RAAF
Flying Officer R.E. Barnlund, RCAF
Flying Officer G.C. Brickwood, RCAF
Flying Officer K.B. Woodhouse, RCAF
Sgt. K.E. Lussier, RCAF
1st Lt. W.B. Lock, USAAF
1st Lt. M.L. Rosenblatt, USAAF
1st Lt. M.V. Shevchik, USAAF
2nd Lt. A.T. Coffman, Jr., USAAF
2nd Lt. W.A. Hoffman III, USAAF
2nd Lt. R.V Laux, USAAF
2nd Lt. J.M. Thorson, USAAF
2nd Lt. P.T. Wright, USAAF
Tech. Sgt. R.J. Rujawitz, USAAF
Staff Sgt. J.F. Bernier, USAAF
Staff Sgt. G.P. Buckner, USAAF
Staff Sgt. D.G. Helsel, USAAF
Staff Sgt. C.H. Mullins, USAAF
Staff Sgt. K.W. Sutor, USAAF
Staff Sgt. R.H. Sweatt, USAAF
Sgt. R. Cutino, USAAF
Sgt. T.J. Glennan, USAAF
Sgt. R.C. Hamilton, USAAF
Sgt. A.A. Helfgott, USAAF
Sgt. F.C. Wall, USAAF
Sgt. D. Warner, USAAF

Opération Crozier I, 12-13 July 1944

Flt. Lt. L.W.F. Stark, RAF
Sgt. A. Elder, RAF
Sgt. R.J. Dickson, RAF
Flying Officer H.J. Brennan, RCAF
Pilot Officer A.J. Houston, RCAF
Sgt. E.J. Trottier, RCAF
Sub Lt. M.I.G. Hamilton, RNVR
Leading Seaman A.H. Dellow, RNVR
Ordinary Seaman H.D. Rockwood, RNVR
1st Lt. R.C. Gordon, USAAF
1st Lt. F.L. Lee, USAAF
2nd Lt. W.C. Hawkins, USAAF
2nd Lt. J.A. Lilly, USAAF

Opération Crozier II, 24-25 July 1944

Sqdn. Ldr. P.H. Smith, RAF
Flt. Sgt. T.P. Fargher, RAF
Maj. O.A.J. Cary-Elwes, SAS
Sgt. E. Mills, SAS
Maj. W.A. Jones, USAAF

Note: This list does not include non-military evacuees (Val Williams, Ivan the Russian, Jean Gicquel, Jean Tréhiou and his fellow French agents).

It takes little imagination to understand the sublime quality of the courage that, during Hitler's occupation of France, dedicated French citizens displayed in undertaking to rescue Allied fliers downed over France. They undertook the work deliberately and with the certain knowledge that they were risking not only their own lives but those of all they held dear.

This they did far from the excitement and frenzy of the battlefield: their inspiration was their patriotism, the determination to see their beloved country freed from the domination of the hated Nazis and by their ideals of liberty and justice that they shared with the Allied fliers who were risking their own lives each time they made a sortie into Europe.

The loss of each Allied plane that was shot down over Europe was a tragedy. Every member of a crew that was found and saved and sent back to us throughout "Operation Bonaparte" brought joy to all his comrades.

To every Frenchman who joined in this great work and to each member of his family and to all who shared in those days, his risks and dangers, I send assurances of my deep and lasting gratitude.

—Dwight Eisenhower, in a personal thank you to the Ropers Family.

PART II

FURTHER ACCOUNTS

In the course of researching the Shelburne Line, I came across further, intensely personal accounts of the war in France. Some were of downed airmen; others were of ordinary French people caught up in the war. Some were connected to Plouha and the Shelburne Line, some were not. But all were stories I felt deserved to be told, and they comprise the second part of this book. Several accounts are about friends, either in France or the United States, whom it has been a pleasure and an honor to know.

My granddad told me stories
Of a time he knew firsthand,
How people fought to build a home
In a new but hostile land.
My father sailed the ocean
Throughout the Second World War
And fought to make this world a place
Of peace forever more ...

Now there are men I've come to know,
Brave heroes tried and true.
Men like Patton, Eisenhower,
And Doug MacArthur, too.
They fought for peace and won the fight,
As you can plainly see,
Each time you look outside and see
The children running free.

So now our generation
Has grown older and I pray
The things we teach our children
Will guide them along life's way.
For some day we'll die and our names will fall
Down history's deep dark well
And though we're gone we'll still live
In tales old-timers tell.

From " HEROES," by Jack A. Mueller, ©1976

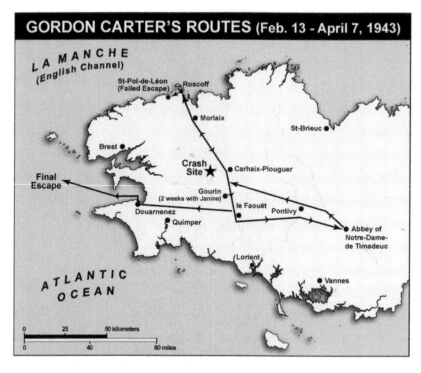

GORDON CARTER'S ROUTES (Feb. 13 - April 7, 1943)

LA MANCHE
(English Channel)

St-Pol-de-Léon
(Failed Escape)
Roscoff
Morlaix
St-Brieuc
Brest
Crash
Site
Carhaix-Plouguer
Final
Escape
Gourin
(2 weeks with Janine)
le Faouët
Pontivy
Douarnenez
Abbey of
Notre-Dame-
de Timadeuc
Quimper
Lorient
Vannes
ATLANTIC
OCEAN

0   25   50 kilometers
0   40   80 miles

*Gordon Carter in
his RAF uniform.*

CHAPTER 9

SPIRIT OF THE RESISTANCE
GORDON CARTER

It was the day-to-day behavior of ordinary people doing something they
didn't have to do, but did, that made up the spirit of the Resistance.
—Gordon Carter

*In 2008, my husband Don and I were visiting our friends Floh and Klaus
Kroemer in the Breton village of Guilvinec, 80 miles south-west of Plouha on
the coast of Finisterre. We were telling them, over dinner, about our research
on the Shelburne Line and the book we proposed to write.*

*"We've heard there's a Canadian World War II aviator who lives
somewhere around here with his French wife," Floh and Klaus told us.
"He supposedly crashed and was saved by a family here in Brittany." They
suggested that his war experience and illustrious post-war career as a United
Nations diplomat warranted inclusion in our book. "We'll try to locate him so
you can interview him."*

*Two years later, we made contact with Gordon Carter and his French wife,
Janine Jouanjean. They agreed to meet us in their apartment in Quimper, a
Breton city between Guilvinec and Brest. Getting to Quimper was no problem,
but our car was armed with a GPS that voiced incorrect directions, no matter
which way we circled round the city. As the minutes became an hour, I stopped
at a construction site to ask directions. The foreman began explaining, then
stopped. "Ah . . . it's too complicated," he told me in French. "I'll take my truck.
You follow me."*

He left his wife—who was dressed in a scarf and tunic—in charge. "Hmm good," I thought to myself, "she's an emancipated woman."

The man hopped into his gravel truck and led us out of the site. We followed him for fifteen, twenty minutes. Finally the truck stopped. Don and I waited while the driver got out, came over to our car, and pointed to the entry drive, marked with the name of the apartment complex where the Carters lived. We thanked the man profusely and asked if he would accept some money for his service. "No, no," he said. "You're Americans. We appreciate you." What kindness—I fought back tears as we said au revoir to the man.

Don and I arrived two hours late for our interview. Despite the delay, the Carters received us graciously and we spent a delightful remainder of the afternoon recording Gordon's story. The following account is based on our interview, ensuing telephone conversations, correspondence, and Gordon's privately published Memories of War. [1]

English-born Gordon Carter and his family had been residents of the United States for five years when the war broke out in Europe. The United States remained firmly neutral at this time, but Canada declared war on Germany shortly after Great Britain and France, in September 1939, when Gordon was just sixteen.

Two years later, at the end of his sophomore year at Dartmouth College, Gordon abandoned his studies and crossed the border to Canada to follow the "call of duty." He signed up for a Canadian Scots ambulance unit bound for Singapore, but was turned down due to his age. Although disappointed, he soon learned that the entire unit was captured a few months later when Singapore fell to the Japanese.

Upon his 18th birthday, he applied to the Royal Canadian Air Force (RCAF) and was accepted. He passed his initial tests with high grades and in the winter of 1941, he was sent to the Maritime Provinces for navigation and flight instruction.

After eleven months of intensive training as a bombardier/navigator Gordon received his commission as a Flying Officer. The report of his commanding officer read, "This man knows his navigation and exploits it to the nth degree."

Sent to England in June 1942, Gordon, now 19, joined the RAF's

---

1 Housed at the Imperial War Museum in Duxford, England.

No. 35 Squadron, part of the elite Pathfinder Force. The Pathfinders took their name from the fact that, at night, they dropped target-indicator incendiaries (TIs) over a bombing objective to light the target area for the bombers that followed.

On February 13, 1943, during Gordon's thirteenth mission (one of the fifty-one missions in which he took part), his Halifax bomber was hit over Lorient, France. Their target had been one of the five German U-Boat bases located along the French Atlantic Coast.[2] The Germans had so heavily fortified the bunkers that Allied bombs proved ineffective in penetrating the twelve-foot-thick reinforced concrete walls. The Allies were aware of this, so the purpose of the Lorient raid was to destroy the harbor and any of the city's support facilities that supplied materials and equipment for the Germans.

The 35 Squadron had taken off from its RAF base in England earlier in the evening, crossed the English Channel and flown directly south across Brittany. Just after 2100 hours, the Pathfinders lined up over Lorient and began releasing their TIs, along with three 1000-pound bombs from each plane. Gordon's four-engine Halifax, carrying a crew of seven, had just dropped its incendiaries, when an explosion shook the plane.

"Bail out! Bail out! Hit by flak," came the pilot's order. With one engine on fire and flames streaming aft, Gordon prepared to jump first so as to clear the way for the rest of the crew. His training had not included actual parachute jumps so it was a good test of his mettle.

Bailing out is quite a proposition, he told Don and me. *But we had no choice, and I had to go out first because the port [left] engine was on fire. Rather unknowingly, I delayed jumping, because if you've ever jumped with a parachute at night and in a burning aircraft, you're not too keen to do it.*

I had to release my seat, which was on a spring, grab my parachute off a rack, hook it onto my parachute harness, remove the hatch cover and throw it into the nose of the aircraft so the wind couldn't jam it as I exited. All this time, while the plane is spinning out of control, the centrifugal force pins you against the sides, making it difficult to move at all. But somehow you get your feet through the hole and, facing backwards, you call to the pilot, "Bailing out, bailing out."

Then, at the last minute before you go out, you remove your helmet so

---

2 The others were Brest, St. Nazaire, La Rochelle and Bordeaux.

RAF Halifax Bomber, WWII.

Carter's Halifax bomber, on the ground in France.

that neither the oxygen tube nor the intercom strangles you, and with the hand that's holding you in place against the rim of the hatch opening, you let go. Your boots finally come out and before you know it, you've passed the tail and pulled the ripcord. I went down thoroughly grateful to be on the end of a parachute. The descent was silent, motionless and beautiful on that moonlit night. And, as I came down those 10,000 feet, I could hear a voice below me calling me. I plunged into the arms of a young man who said, "Tu es mon frère." (You are my brother.)

Gordon stopped at this point during our interview. He leaned over in his chair, took a breath and tried to resume his account. But his voice broke and tears streamed down his cheeks. Clearly, the memory was still extremely poignant sixty-seven years later.

Somewhere in the moonlight, in the ploughed field, Gordon sighted fellow crewmember, aircraft gunner Napoleon (Nap) Barry, a French-Canadian. Both men had landed on the south side of the Nantes-to-Brest Canal in central Brittany. (Unbeknownst to them, the rest of their crew had landed north of the canal, where they were rescued by Georges (Geo) Jouanjean, chief of Oaktree—the Breton section of the Pat O'Leary Line that had been organized by Val Williams.)

In Gordon and Nap's case, the young man belonging to the "voice" gathered their parachutes, buried them and, in the dark, led them to an old farmhouse. There the two men were offered food, local cider and clothes. Gordon had prepared for such an eventuality and wore a layer of civilian clothes underneath his battle dress; Nap had not and gladly accepted what was offered—farmers' coveralls, a worker's hat and work shoes. The two men were something of a local attraction that night, particularly Gordon with his wavy hair, dimpled face and six-foot stature. People came from neighboring farms with gifts of home-made cider or wine for *"les Anglais"*—an indication that their "rescuers" were ordinary people who lacked the training and discipline of an organized Resistance group. This naïve behavior could easily have compromised the airmen, their rescuers and the neighbors as well.

The following morning, after a cramped night in a *Gwele Kloz*, [a "closet bed," Breton for a bed similar to a Murphy bed] Gordon and Nap set out from the farmhouse on foot.[3] They walked until dusk. Exhausted and with swollen feet, they decided they should try to spend the night indoors somewhere. They knocked on the door of a farmhouse, told the farmer they were Canadian aviators, and asked if he could put them up for the night. He let them enter only after they had shown him their dog tags. "If you'd been English, I would have refused," he told them.

Gordon and Nap were taken aback by the farmer's comment. The two were unaware that, after the Vichy French government signed the Armistice with Germany on June 22, 1940, Britain had ordered the destruction of the French naval fleet that lay docked at Mers-el-Kébir in Algeria. Fearing the ships would fall into German hands, the British had sent an ultimatum to the French Naval Minister, Admiral Darlan, requiring that the fleet become part of the Royal Navy forces or else be deactivated in some way. The French refused the ultimatum and, on July 3, the British began the destruction of the fleet. One battleship was sunk, five other ships were damaged, and almost 1,300 French lives were lost. Because of this, many French—particularly Bretons, who comprised the majority of French sailors—harbored a fierce animosity toward the British.[4]

The following morning the farmer accompanied Gordon and Nap to a nearby village to catch an interurban bus to the town of Pontivy. From there, they hoped to escape to the south of France, then across the Pyrenees to Spain and eventually to the British base in Gibraltar.

Gordon recalled, *When I saw how full the bus was, I realized we wouldn't get aboard; so I made a calculated risk. I went right up to the driver, told him we were English airmen, and that we had to get to Spain.*

"Get in," he said, shoving us in and locking the door. A man near the door who overheard us—another gamble on our part—told us that when we got to Pontivy we should go to the Grand Café and ask for Pierre Valy, the owner, and a man named Guy, which we did.

After we'd been waiting for a while in the cafe, a man entered carrying a cage with a ferret in it. The man, Guy Lenfant—code-named Dubreuil—told

---

3 Years later, Gordon and his wife Janine found the house where the farmer had hidden the two men. Two of the daughters—youngsters in 1943—remembered Gordon. They showed him a teapot, kept as a precious souvenir, in which their mother had hidden a report about his and Nap's sojourn.
4 See Jackson, pp 129-129, *France the Dark Years;* Winston S. Churchill, *Never Give In,* pp. 229-234.

us he was a French agent whose job was to organize the parachute drops of arms and ammunitions for Resistance groups.[5] He said he would take us on as extras because there was no way to get us out of the country at this time.

Glancing around to make sure there were no Germans in the café, Guy set his cage on the counter and called the ferret by its name, "Hitler." He reached into the cage and lifted up the ferret's bed of straw. The bottom of the cage concealed a stash of French bills.

"I don't need a bank account," he whispered quietly, "The ferret looks after my money." This was definitely a case of reality being stranger than fiction!

For the next two weeks, Gordon and Nap helped Guy transport arms and ammunition dropped by parachute for the local Resistance groups.

Guy's practice was always to do the very thing you wouldn't expect him to do. For example, one day we were cycling through a nearby town when a crowd of German soldiers poured out of a movie theater. "This is the safest place to be," he told us. "They won't suspect somebody who's mixing with the crowd, but if you try to sneak around the back of the theater, that's a signal you're trying to hide." On another occasion, we went into a café full of German soldiers to have an ersatz coffee [imitation coffee, made with chicory]. Guy walked right up to one of them, took the soldier's rifle out of his hands and, mocking an inspection of arms, began to dismantle the gun, making all sorts of remarks the soldier didn't understand. But the soldier thought it was great fun, and soon all the other Germans were laughing, too.

Through his radio operator, Guy arranged for Gordon and Nap to be picked up by a Royal Navy boat at St. Pol-de-Léon on the north coast of Brittany, a distance of over sixty miles from Pontivy. The three men hired a taxi to take them to the limit of the coastal zone, beyond which further travel was restricted without a pass. They then walked nine miles to Morlaix where they caught a train to their destination.

On arrival, they picked up an American they nicknamed "Petit Pierre," a rangy Texan who, at 6'4", towered over everyone else, including Gordon. His real name was Lieutenant Robert Biggs, and he claimed to be from the USAAF 367 Squadron, based at Thurleigh, near Gordon's home airfield at Graveley.

---

5 Lenfant was an agent of the Gaulliste bureau (BOA—*Bureau d'Opérations Aériennes*) in London charged with making parachute drops of arms, munitions and equipment for the Underground. The money, destined for Resistance agents, was part of a recent parachute drop from MI-9 in London.

Guy told me that if I was satisfied "Petit Pierre" was genuine he could join us. But if I weren't sure, Guy would have to eliminate him. Shocked, I had to make up my mind quickly. I had recently visited the Thurleigh Air Base in England, so I knew some of its features. I pulled the giant aside, interrogated him and determined that his facts were legitimate. Otherwise, I wouldn't have known what questions to ask, and Guy would have taken him into the woods and shot him on the spot.

Impulsive and not knowing a word of French, Petit Pierre proved to be a bit of a challenge to the three other men, aside from the issue of his height.

At St. Pol we had to go through German military control before we could exit the train station. Petit Pierre followed right behind me. The German sentry started to pull him aside and the Texan raised his arm to throw a punch. Immediately, Guy grabbed his arm and held it down. That would have been the end of all of us, since none of us had a German Military Customs permit [Ausweis]. Fortunately, the French official in the station office issued us a temporary permit with no questions asked.

The four men stopped at the hotel where Guy's radio operator was closeted. They waited for the BBC radio message confirming that a boat would arrive that night to pick them up. After dark Guy, Nap, Petit Pierre and Gordon set out on rented bicycles for the designated cove. Cycling along the coastal roads, each man armed with a revolver, was a risky game and they soon faced a dangerous test.

It wasn't long before we ran up against two French gendarmes who started making trouble. Guy let them rant for a while, then said, "Stop fooling around. You're two, and we're four. We're all armed so if you start the shooting you know what the result will be." The two gendarmes calmed down and agreed to let us go.

A little further on the group came to a house where a party was taking place. The four men could hear the clinking of glasses and loud German voices shouting *"Prost."* Then, as they were passing the gate to the house, a sentry called out, *"Halt!"*

Guy Lenfant didn't waste any time. Operating on the theory that if you talk, you talk first and don't stop talking, he laid into the German sentry with a mixture of languages and somehow got him so sentimental about the German defeat at Stalingrad that he sent us on our way without any further problems.

The terrain grew sandier as the four men made their way across fields to the cove where they expected to be picked up. Small willow trees, brushy hedges and a large rock in the middle of the beach corresponded exactly to the details given in the BBC message.

Exhausted and cold, the men forced themselves to stay awake, waiting, searching the horizon, but never sighting anything that looked like a surfboat. As it happened, there were two almost-identical coves at that location; the surfboat put into one of them (the wrong one), Guy and the three airmen were in the other. Discouraged, the four men cycled back before dawn to St. Pol-de-Léon and took the return train to Pontivy. By this time, Guy had spent almost three weeks dealing with the aviators—more time than he'd anticipated. He told them, "Look, enough is enough. I have to get on with my work."

He took us to a Trappist monastery in central Brittany that would house aviators without any questions for up to two weeks.[6] After that, "guests" had to clear out. Trappists aren't allowed to speak, so we spent eight days cloistered in cells in semi-darkness, hearing the monks chant all night. That made a big impression on Nap and me—it was calming—but Petit Pierre had a difficult time keeping his mouth shut.

After eight days, *le Père Supérieur* (the Father Superior)—the only monk allowed to speak—told Gordon that someone had come to call for them. This was Georges (Geo) Jouanjean, chief of the Oaktree Line, the Breton section of the Pat O'Leary Line. Gordon, Nap, Petit Pierre and three other Americans who had been cloistered with them left the monastery with Geo, who led them to his Morlaix, then accompanied them aboard the train to Paris.

In Paris, Geo's plan was to deposit the aviators at a safe house where Resistance agents would interrogate them and prepare their false ID cards. After that, they would be returned to Brittany for possible evacuation to England. The six men waited in a nearby café while Geo went ahead to make sure the way was clear. He suddenly reappeared. Arriving at the appointed address in Paris, he had found the door sealed with yellow tape,

---

6 Abbaye Notre-Dame de Timadeuc is located along the Canal Nantes to Brest, south of Loudéac. The Germans kept a blind eye to the monastery until late in the war when they arrested the Father Superior, Father Guénaël, and deported him to Buchenwald, where he died in 1945. A cross, erected on the hill above the Abbey, commemorates Father Guénaël's courage.

meaning the Gestapo had paid the house a visit.

Without another delivery address for his "packages," Geo spent the day leading the young men around Paris. To help pass the time before nightfall, he sneaked them into a movie theater where, surrounded by German soldiers, they watched a French comedy. Gordon and Nap, who understood the film and laughed along with the rest of the audience, had to keep Petit Pierre under constant watch. Nudging Gordon's arm repeatedly he would ask, "What're they saying? What're they saying?"

Exasperated and worried that one of the Germans would hear the Texan, Gordon finally muttered through clenched teeth, "Shut up and don't say another word."

After twenty-four hours without food, Geo applied Guy Lenfant's principle of outrageous audacity. He chose a restaurant on the Champs-Elysées. *It was crowded with German officers and their lady friends, whereas the four of us in our crumpled suits didn't even have a meal ration coupon between us. On the quiet, Geo told the young waiter our predicament—"no money, no ration coupons"—and we were served as fine a meal as you could get in Paris in 1943.*

Around midnight that evening the group boarded the train back to Brittany. Gordon wondered who was paying for their tickets.

Back in Brittany, Geo made arrangements to place the men separately in safe houses. He convinced his 21-year-old sister, Janine Jouanjean, to help him deliver the three English aviators. "I want you to come with us," he told her. "It looks less suspicious to have a girl with us in case we meet a German." Janine agreed to help and, during the 15-mile (24 km) bicycle ride to their "delivery" point, Gordon made a first and lasting impression on the lovely blue-eyed blond by repairing the leaks in her aging bicycle tires.

Gordon was housed with Janine's sister and brother-in-law in the town of Gourin, 40 miles (64 km) south-west of St Brieuc, and for the next two weeks he and Janine were inseparable. They took long walks in the country. They bicycled. They went to movies among German soldiers. They ran errands to search for bread and sugar. No one bothered them.

"Looking back, it was madness," Janine told me. "The two of us alone, in a place occupied by Germans. But I was never afraid."

How did her mother feel, I wondered? Janine replied that her mother didn't know what they were doing. "She lived in Morlaix; I lived in Carhaix. But like so many families then, she didn't ask questions. I'm sure she suspected that Geo was working for the Resistance, but she never said a word. Besides, as young people, and living in the country, we really ignored the risk. "

How old was Janine at that time, I asked her. "Twenty-one," she answered with a mischievous smile, "But I was *much* more naïve than even a girl of thirteen is today."

In their two weeks together the couple fell deeply in love.

By the beginning of April 1943, Gordon had been in "hiding" for nearly two months. One evening Geo told him of a daring scheme that might get him back to England. Would he be willing to hijack a new German motor torpedo boat and help drive it across the Channel?

Gordon decided to chance it. The boat was currently undergoing sea trials in Douarnenez, a port town on the west coast of Brittany. That evening after an emotional *au revoir* with Janine and her family, Gordon departed with Geo. The next day, he attended a secret meeting with a group of young Frenchmen at an apartment in Douarnenez to discuss evacuation ideas. Gordon was the sole Englishman and the only aviator. The others wanted to volunteer for De Gaulle's Free French Forces in London.

The hijack idea was dismissed as too risky, and a Breton fisherman volunteered his derelict fishing vessel, a *pinasse*, as a get-away vessel for the seventeen men. He chose twenty-one-year-old Louis (Lili) Marec as its skipper. The boat in question, the *Dalc'h Mad*, was a typical Breton fishing vessel: 36 feet (10 m) in length with a flat hull, a short main mast stepped forward of center, a forestaysail and a small inboard engine. The young Marec, who had fished with his father since childhood, knew the coast well, was immune to seasickness, and was as eager to get to London as the rest of his potential passengers.

The men who had agreed to rendezvous at a specified time on the evening of April 7, 1943 slipped down to the quay, in twos and threes, avoiding German sentries. By curfew that night all seventeen had managed to sneak aboard the *Dalc'h Mad*, where they kept perfectly silent below deck. At dawn, with the tide high, Lili started the engine and motored out

Breton port (Binic) at low tide.

of the inner harbor. So far, so good, but before the boat could move out to the open sea it would have to make it past the two German Military officials guarding the outer harbor.

Breton ports have the highest tide levels in Europe. Exiting or entering an inner harbor must be carried out at high tide when the locks that regulate the harbor open and the seawater levels—both inside and out—reach equilibrium. During the German Occupation, any boat leaving a harbor was required to stop and undergo a search. The men well knew that any *"terroristes"* who were found faced execution by hanging or firing squad.

To prevent the German officials from boarding *Dalc'h Mad*, Lili and several of his friends had concocted a plot. A few yards from the quayside, Lili brought the *pinasse* to a stop and idled the engine, as if waiting for the Germans to board. Meanwhile, two of his friends came down to the guardhouse complaining that they had been called to repair the electric lighting along the quay. They had no time to waste, they said, and they needed the two officials to deal with the issue immediately.

A moment later, another friend of Lili's showed up complaining that someone had stolen the tarp he used to cover his car each night, and could the officers please come to investigate the "theft" (which he had carried out himself).

By this time, with Lili and two of his "crewmen" aboard the *Dalc'h Mad* shouting at the Germans to hurry before the tide changed, and the three other men on shore yelling at them as well, the officials were overwhelmed. "*Raus!*" they shouted, and motioned the boat to move out. Lili slammed the throttle into forward gear and the vessel chugged out to sea.

By dark that night, *Dalc'h Mad* had cleared land. But hour upon hour, the wind intensified and soon the boat was riding out a raging storm. Rolling violently from side to side and pitching stern to bow with every wave, the seventeen men aboard wondered if they would survive drowning, let alone make it to England. As saltwater and vomit sloshed over them in the hold, someone remarked that the pinasse had been well named: *Dalc'h Mad* in Breton means "Hold On!"

Lili was unaffected by the motion of the sea and remained on deck, manning the helm. The storm raged on, and by the middle of the night the boat appeared to be coming apart. Water entered every seam of the hull. Pumping had no effect. Seawater kept flooding in. To minimize strain on the seams, Lili turned the boat into the wind while the men frantically tried to block the leaks. Nothing they did seemed to help until, suddenly, Lili had an idea. Removing the staysail from the forestay, he nailed the canvas sail over the center of the hull. The leaks slowed and eventually the storm abated as well, to the relief of all on board. By this time, they had been at sea for three days.

Lili kept the boat heading north for another twenty-four hours. Finally, they sighted what seemed to be the coast of England—Gordon identified St. Michael's Mount, a tiny island off the southwest coast of Cornwall.

Soon afterward, Gordon said, *we ran into a crabbing boat—a Cornish fisherman from a coastal village who told us we were heading in the right direction. Lili gave him all our surplus fuel in exchange for his leading us through a minefield, and we arrived safely at the Lizard Point Lifeboat Ramp* [on the southernmost point of Cornwall]. *As we entered the little cove and anchored off the ramp, the locals cheered and shouted enthusiastically. Soon, rowboats from shore delivered sandwiches, little homemade cakes and tea, such as we hadn't seen for months.*

Gordon was the first of the seventeen men to be allowed ashore, so that British officials could verify that he was truly part of the RAF Pathfinders, as he claimed. After that, telegrams were sent to his family and to his squadron confirming he was alive. *I was put in a first-class carriage on the train to London. No socks, salt in my hair, a tattered suit and looking totally disreputable. But not one of the passengers as much as looked at me, let alone said anything or asked anything. In war anything can happen.* In London, he was grilled again for days by the military, as well as by MI-9. Asked if he would return to Brittany as an agent for the Resistance, Gordon declined. He was afraid of compromising Janine and her family. He asked instead to rejoin his squadron, and he began bombing missions again shortly afterwards.

His young French companions were delivered to French authorities for intensive interrogation. All sixteen, who succeeded in convincing the authorities of their dedication, underwent training with De Gaulle's FFL.

Two months later, in June 1943, unbeknownst to Gordon, Janine's brother, Geo Jouanjean, was caught in a Gestapo trap as the Pat O'Leary Line and its Oaktree branch in Brittany were infiltrated. Geo was arrested and tortured in French prisons for the next nine months, but he never revealed any information. He was then sent to a series of German concentration camps but he survived these further ordeals. After his liberation by the Americans in April 1945, he was awarded five different decorations for his role as a member of the French Underground and for delivering to safety more than 60 British and American airmen—including Gordon Carter.

Gordon himself was shot down a second time, during his 51st bombing operation, on February 20, 1944—the date the Allies began a massive bombing campaign of Germany. He was captured and sent to an *Oflag* where he remained until the camp was liberated, in May 1945. Upon his release, he immediately contacted Janine Jouanjean and she accepted his proposal of marriage. The Carters stayed initially in France, where Gordon worked for the Save the Children Fund. From the late 1940s until his retirement in 1980, he held a variety of international postings with UNICEF. He took great personal satisfaction in the designation of 1979, the year before his retirement, as the International Year of the Child.

In June 2012, the Carters celebrated their 67th wedding anniversary in Quimper, France, where they lived after Gordon's retirement. Gordon kept in touch, supplying a number of photographs, reliable sources of information, and additional contacts for this book until his death in 2013. It has been an honor for me to know the Carters.

Gordon and Janine after the war.

Gordon Carter speaking at a Resistance commemoration, c. 2000. Though not a Shelburne evacuee, he said: "On the cliff top, beholding the coastline where these operations took place, shrouded in wintry mist or bathed in summer sunshine, we are taken back fifty years and we live anew, in silence and for a fleeting moment, an epic which is now legendary." "

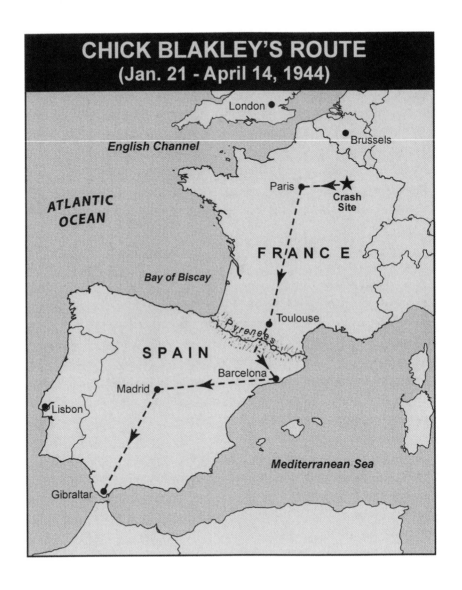

CHICK BLAKLEY'S ROUTE
(Jan. 21 - April 14, 1944)

London

Brussels

English Channel

ATLANTIC
OCEAN

Paris

Crash
Site

F R A N C E

Bay of Biscay

Toulouse

Pyrenees

S P A I N

Barcelona

Madrid

Lisbon

Mediterranean Sea

Gibraltar

124

CHAPTER 10

A MILK RUN MISSION
CHICK BLAKLEY

In April 2011, I received an unexpected packet in the mail from Charles (Chick) W. Blakley. He was a WWII aviator from Idaho who had been shot down in north-east France in January, 1944. Included in the packet were a copy of his false French ID, photos and articles about the crash of his plane, and his subsequent evasion and rescue. His "gift" to me was in response to a request for information that I had placed in the Air Forces Escape and Evasion Society (AFEES) newsletter. Since sending that initial packet, Chick has kept in touch through email and the postal service, correcting errors and omissions in this chapter, and sending additional information he finds appropriate as he "digs" through his memorabilia.

At 1100 hours (11:00 a.m.) on January 21, 1944—seven days before Lucien Dumais received word from MI-9 that the first Bonaparte Operation was scheduled—the 66th and 68th Bomb Squadrons took off in their B-24s from their base at Shipdham, in Norfolk, England. The airmen had been briefed earlier in the morning that their mission for the day was just "a milk run"—a short, routine outing. Their target was to be the Nazi V-1 Buzz Bomb Launch site near Calais, in northeastern France, across the narrowest part of English Channel. They were expected to drop their bombs within an hour or two and return to the base by late afternoon.

Twenty-two year old Sergeant Chick (Charles) Blakley from Parma,

Chick Blakley in uniform.

The crew of the 'Ram It-Dam It.' Chick Blakley is at lower left.

Idaho was flying that day as left waist gunner on his eighth mission. The squadron was flying low, at about 12,000 feet, but cloud cover was so heavy that the lead plane of their twelve-ship group could not locate the target. The bomb site, located at Escalles-sur-Buchy, was difficult to locate even in good weather, however, as it was highly camouflaged with turf. At 1515 hours (3:15 p.m.), as Chick's plane, the "Ram It-Dam It," circled to make its fifth attempt, German Me 109 fighters blasted into action, attacking the plane and hitting engines number three and four. Flames immediately enveloped the flight deck.

I started toward the deck with an extinguisher, Chick wrote, *but the flames had already enveloped the cabin. The other four rear crewmen had already bailed out. I put on my chute and started toward the flight deck with a fire extinguisher but decided I'd better leave too. I delayed for five or six thousand feet before pulling my rip cord and tumbled viciously at first, then slowed and floated on my back. As I neared the ground a large tree was beneath me, so I pulled some chute cords to drift from it and next thing I knew the ground hit me very hard.*

Chick landed outside the village of Poix, about 30 miles (50 km) southeast of Amiens. He took off his chute, gathered it up in a ball and stashed it in the bushes. He took off into the woods where he hid in a thicket near the trail. *I saw two people approaching. One was a woman. The second was Archie Barlow, our engineer. I called out to him and the French woman who had rescued him almost had a heart attack. Gesturing excitedly to keep quiet, she hid us both in a haystack and, using sign language, promised to return after dark at 2100 hours to take us to her home.*

While Chick and Archie waited, it began to pour rain. They could hear German search parties patrolling the area, obviously looking for survivors. The soldiers sloshed through mud and puddles, swearing and muttering in their guttural language. Finally the voices stopped.

At the appointed hour, the woman returned to find the two Americans drenched and happy to be taken to her house. There they found two more members of their crew: radio operator, Alvin Rosenblatt, and gunner, Alfred Klein. Chick and Archie learned that two further members of their crew had been captured and taken as POWs. A fifth member—a cameraman—had evaded capture but took off on his own and lost contact with the three others. Tragically, the parachute of the pilot had failed to open and the rest of the flight deck crew—co-pilot, navigator and bombardier—had gone down with the aircraft.

Within two days, the woman had the men outfitted in civilian clothing. For Chick, who was tall and had feet to match, finding shoes that were large enough (size 13) was a problem. The only ones that came close to fitting were a pair of patent leather oxfords. Chick would struggle with these shoes for the next six weeks.

The local Underground soon arranged for the men's lodgings in Paris and, within less than a week, they were transferred into the care of further Underground members and taken from Poix by train to the capital. The group was split up and hidden with various families around the city. Chick was separated from his fellow crew members and found himself sharing a small room above a bakery with an RAF Spitfire pilot named Bill, whose plane had been shot down in northeastern France as he strafed a German freight train. The baker's wife delivered fresh bread and coffee to the two men each morning, but only when the bakery closed for the night were they allowed to join the family downstairs. Upstairs and alone during the daytime, the airmen reasoned that if they were ever to get out of France they would have to do a lot of foot travel. In preparation, they spent most of their day doing push-ups and sit-ups to stay in shape. It also helped them pass the time. When Chick finally returned to his Bomb Group, his commanding officer was astonished to learn that he and Bill had been doing "calisthenics," as these exercises were performed daily by all personnel in uniform and were just as routinely loathed.

To avoid jeopardizing either the lodgers or their host families, all of the airmen were moved frequently. After two weeks above the bakery, Chick and Bill were placed on the fifth floor of a Paris apartment with a family who made a trip each weekend to a farm and returned each Sunday night with sacks of food and vegetables for all of the hidden men. Neither Chick nor Bill realized what terrible risks the family was taking to obtain and deliver these supplies. On week nights, after dark, individual family members also took turns walking each man around the neighborhood for exercise. Although neither aviator knew exactly where they were, in the larger cities, including Paris, they memorized the names of the streets where their host families lived, and later, during interrogation by MI-9 in London, they would report these addresses.

Chick Blakley's false ID.

While the men waited and the Resistance families sheltered and fed them, clandestine photographers and forgers worked as fast as they could to create new identities. On March 1, six weeks after his crash, Chick Blakley became "Gaston Louis Humbert," a mechanic from Caen. Chick had curly hair and a blond complexion, meaning that he looked nothing like the typical young Frenchmen of those days, who tended to be shorter than North Americans and have black stubble on their faces; but the new ID meant that Chick could begin his attempt to leave France.

That same evening, in company of four other airmen and four French guides, Chick and Bill boarded an overnight train to Toulouse, in the south of France on the edge of the Pyrenees. The men were not aware of the existence of organized escape lines, nor that several of these—the Pat O'Leary Line from Marseille, the Comet Line from Toulouse—had been compromised in the preceding months, with many of their helpers arrested by the Gestapo and executed or sent to concentration camps in Germany. The airmen knew only that each new place they went, there were people who assisted them.

In Toulouse, with the aviator count now fourteen, we were hidden during the daytime in a public library where we stuck out like a sore thumb. That evening we boarded a southbound train and, we were told that, as it slowed for the station at the small village of Foix, we were to jump out on the opposite side of the station platform. With a sense of humor and a feeling for the sound of the French language, Chick added, *So our French train rides had started at Poix* [Pwa] *and ended at Foix* [Fwa].

The fourteen airmen crouched along the railroad tracks at Foix until all traffic had disappeared, then set out on an all-night walk. It was 55 miles to the foothills of the Pyrenees, and Chick was still wearing his ill-fitting patent leather shoes. For the next five days a snowstorm raged in the mountains, forcing the men and their guides to hole up in a barn.

To keep warm, we made a long bed in the hay, each man lying barefoot to the armpit of the next. One of the guides covered us with hay and a tarpaulin, then dug a hole for himself and crawled in. This had to be done with the last light of day and we had to stay covered till daylight, not budging one inch. We got very stiff lying in one position!

For food, the guides bought a sheep from a farmer and boiled it in a huge pot. The only parts not used were the wool and the 'baa', but we were so hungry we didn't complain. It even tasted okay.

On the fifth day, the guides determined the snow had frozen enough to allow for travel and, that night, the airmen began their long trudge up into the mountains. In some places the snowdrifts were as deep as their armpits. They had started at sea level and had 3000 feet (1000 meters) to go. Archie Barlow, the engineer on Chick's plane, found it tough going. He was sick and exhausted and unable to maneuver through the snow, slowing the group so much that the guides advised leaving him in a barn. They ordered him not to return to the French border for three days so as to give the rest of the group time to get out of the area. *Rosenblatt and I left him some rations and matches, but months later I learned that he couldn't start a fire and the corned beef was too frozen to eat.* Archie eventually managed to descend to the valley. There, in a small village, he encountered a French policeman who bought him a train ticket to return to Paris.

The remaining thirteen airmen continued their icy slog upward, in the dark, through continuing snowdrifts. One night their guides led them to an abandoned castle where they were able to build a fire and dry out their clothes. The following night, as they crossed an ice-filled stream along a ridge above a road, the guides stopped abruptly. "Flatten out, flatten out," they motioned. The men dove into the snow. A few hundred feet below they could hear the sound of a German jeep patrol passing by. Had it been daylight, the group could easily have been sighted.

At dawn the next morning, the guides seemed to be searching for something on the mountain. We thought they were lost, but it turned out they'd been looking for an opening to an aqueduct tunnel. They led us into this dark tunnel where we walked for an hour squeezed between the tunnel wall and the water pipe, one shoulder hitting the wall, the other against the pipe bands that tore our jackets. When we exited the tunnel it was daylight and we saw we'd gone through a mountain, instead of having to go over it.

While we rested, the guides pointed to the next summit—indicating that was the border. We had to crawl up the last 200 yards of a glacier on our hands and knees. But at the top we crossed into the tiny principality of Andorra, 181 square miles surrounded by the French and Spanish Pyrenees. At that point, the guides took their leave of us, and began their return to the north. Chick noted that the date was March 13. *We thirteen airmen had traveled for thirteen days from March 1 to March 13. What a lucky number!*

He also paid tribute to the guides and everyone else from Poix onwards who had helped them. *To me, the French Underground was any group of people whose contribution to the war effort was to pass us on to other people they knew and trusted. That was their way of fighting the enemy.*

For the next several days in Andorra the men were lodged in a large room in the company of what Chick called a "United Nations in hiding"—escapees from Germany, France, Britain, and America—all waiting for a final passage to safety. As a prelude to this, Chick's patent leather shoes were replaced with a pair of espadrilles—cloth sandals with hemp soles. *They explained to me that we had another night of walking to bypass the guards on the Andorra-Spanish border, and the espadrilles would keep noise to a minimum. Struggling on up the mountain, I wished that I had my oxfords back for, as we walked across scree-filled snow, sharp rocks worked their way up the soles and into my feet. But we finally made it into Spain the next morning and spent the day in a bar, waiting for someone from the British Embassy to pick us up.*

Finally, an employee of the embassy came for us in a 1934 Ford sedan that burned coke for fuel. It was daylight and, as we looked down on Barcelona, it was the first time we'd seen a city unaffected by the War. No bombed out areas. No destruction. No blackouts. For our British comrades it had been years since they witnessed such a scene.

The British Embassy issued new clothing to each airman, including a two-piece civilian suit—an outfit Chick hadn't worn since his high school prom.

Subjected to physical exams and interrogation, and fed plenty of food in Barcelona, the men were next transferred to Madrid.

They were not able to move everyone in the group at one time, so Rosenblatt and I stayed behind. One Sunday afternoon an Embassy employee took us to a bullfight—an event I'd seen only in photographs.

After we reached Madrid, it was on to Gibraltar, then Casablanca, where we were turned over to an American Military liaison officer—a colonel who smoked roll-your-own Bull Durham cigarettes.

This time, we were issued military uniforms and toilet articles and told to sign forms swearing that we would not tell anyone about our escape story, unless that person was authorized. We were given high priority and, within two days, our 13-man group was the first to board a Liberator transport bound for England. That nine-hour flight seemed like a dream.

In London the airmen were taken to a hospital for physical exams before being sent to MI-9 for yet more interrogation. Chick was treated for a head cold that had infected his ears.

We were issued new uniforms; it was like the first days in the Army, except this time they cared how we looked—they had seamstresses who would alter the uniforms to fit us.

We were told that our ETO [European Theater of Operation] *days of flying were over and that we'd soon be headed back to the United States. The mission they had told us was a "Milk Run" finally ended for those of us who survived.*

On April 14, 1944, nearly three months after his plane went down, newly promoted Tech. Sergeant Charles W. Blakley received his official orders to proceed to the United States. Among the eight other men flying home with him were Sergeant Alvin Rosenblatt, radio operator of the "Ram It-Dam It," and 2nd Lieutenant Ralph Patton, who had been evacuated from Brittany in the third Bonaparte evacuation operation (see Chapter 6). Chick was decorated with a Purple Heart and two Air Medals.

Upon his return to the States, Chick visited his family and then spent two months in a Spokane, Washington, hospital recovering from nervous stress and a foot infection (the latter probably caused by severe frostbite). Following his release from the hospital, he finished his military career as an instructor-supervisor at Chanute Field, Illinois, and later returned to his home state, Idaho, where he lived the remainder of his life.

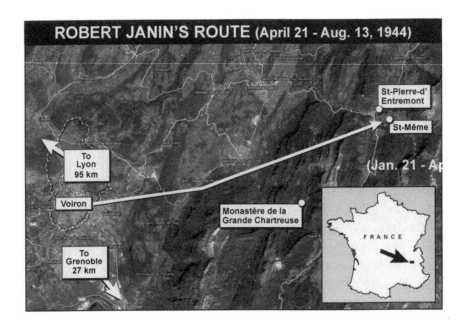

CHAPTER 11

THROUGH THE EYES OF A SIXTEEN-YEAR-OLD
ROBERT JANIN

Les Compagnons de France was one of a number of youth groups authorized by the Vichy government after the defeat of France in 1940. It was a volunteer organization,[1] the purpose of which was ostensibly to train young men from 14 to 19 years old to "work for the Patrie *[Fatherland] and to inculcate good moral values." Many young men opted to attend* Compagnons *training schools to avoid being conscripted to work in Nazi Germany.*

Sixteen-year-old Robert Janin lived in a camp school for the Compagnons *located above Voiron, 40 miles (64 km) northwest of Grenoble, in view of the Chartreuse chain of the Alps. After the War, Robert would marry one of my two adopted French "sisters." In 2011, on his porch overlooking a valley of the Isère River in Savoie, he recounted his story to me for the first time. It was an emotional recalling.*

At eight o'clock on the morning of April 21, 1944, the bell rang at a one-room boys' training camp school in the hills above Voiron. The boys had just sat down at their desks when two Nazi-trained Vichy *Milice* officers, carrying whips in their hands, burst into the room shouting, *"Sortez! Sortez!"*

The teacher nodded quickly to the students, confirming that they

---

1 A stricter, semi-military organization, *Chantiers de la Jeunesse*, was compulsory for 20 year-old French men. *France: The Dark Years*, Julian Jackson.

Robert Janin at 16-17.

should obey the order to move outside. Twenty-five pupils, ages 14 to 19, filed out onto the narrow dirt road that led past the school. "Line up. Line up," the officers demanded. "Smallest first. Tallest last. You, professor, stay there by the door. Do not move."

The orders continued to spill out. "Here, here! You!" the heavier of the two officers shouted at 16-year old Robert Janin. As the shortest of the pupils, Robert was stationed at the front of the line, with a younger, slightly taller boy behind him.

The officer yanked Robert by the arm, drew back his whip, and slapped the ground. *"Vite! Vite! Depéchez-vous!"* (Hurry up!) The second officer shoved the boys into line. "Attention! Stay in line and do not move!"

Pointing to the two-story house across from the school, the first officer shouted, "Who knows that family?" The boys were silent. "Speak!" screamed the first officer. "Who knows that family?" Silence.

Most of the boys knew that the Jourdan family lived in the house, and that an aunt and grandmother lived with them, caring for the Jourdan's two-year old daughter. The boys also knew that the head of the household, Monsieur Jourdan, was head of the local Voiron *Milice*, and that he held frequent meetings that three of the older students attended, posing as "sympathizers."

Robert's 18-year old friend, Colonna, and two others knew, in addition, that the Jourdan's adolescent son carried out missions for the *Milice*. They were also aware that Monsieur Jourdan had participated in the hunt for Resistance members and that he was responsible for the interrogation and execution of local Jewish families.

Like underage Guiguite Le Saux in Plouha, who helped with the Shelburne Line, Robert had been serving as an Underground "mailman," helping Colonna deliver Resistance pamphlets to local mailboxes. Did these Vichy police suspect him? Is that why they were here? Despite his fear, Robert kept his composure.

The *Miliciens* persisted. "Ah, so you won't talk . . . Well then, we will choose two of you to see what has happened." Pulled by the hair, their right arms bent behind their backs, Robert and the second youngster were marched across the road to the Jourdan house. "Stand there," the first officer demanded. He snapped his whip again, bringing it down on Robert's shoulders. Pain shot through the boy's neck and radiated along his spine. He winced and gritted his teeth, without letting out a sound.

The officers opened the door to the house and kicked the two boys inside. "Now . . . take a look and see if you like what you see. . ." The door slammed behind them, the boys were locked in. Outside the house, the teacher and their classmates stood in terrified silence.

Inside the entryway, a long corridor ran the length of the house. To the left was a living-dining room. A large Persian rug covered its hardwood floors, and upholstered chairs surrounded a long mahogany dining table. The two boys entered this room and saw Monsieur Jourdan hunched over the end of the table. Blood from a bullet hole in his neck spewed over the white tablecloth and down onto the rug. An open bottle of green Chartreuse, lay on its side near the man's head, its contents mixed with the blood.

At the back of the room, an open door led into the kitchen. There, on the linoleum floor, lay Madame Jourdan in a pool of dried blood, a broom clutched in her lifeless hand.

"It's beginning to smell in here," Robert said, covering his nose with his hand.

Hoping to escape the odor, the boys crept up the worn oak stairs, expecting to find empty rooms. Instead, they found more horror. On the floor of a large open room with a dark-beamed ceiling, lay an elderly woman with bullet holes in her chest. Along one wall was a bullet-riddled crib containing the body of the Jourdans' infant daughter.

Robert had never seen such a gruesome sight. Everything in the room was a bloody mess. Who could have done this? And why? The two boys went back downstairs and crouched along the wall of the hallway, speechless.

"What do we do now? Will they come back and assassinate *us*?" he wondered. He couldn't speak, not even to say a word to his friend. He just sat there, shaking his head back and forth, back and forth, thinking especially of the baby girl.

As he recounted this story to me six decades later, his voice broke. *"I couldn't believe how anyone could assassinate a baby."* A long pause followed before he was able to resume speaking.

For the next two hours, the boys sat in the hallway, wondering whether they, too, were in line to be executed.

Suddenly, they heard a key being inserted into the front door lock. The two *Milice* officers entered the hallway. "Get up. You can go now. Have you learned a lesson? This is what *terroristes* do to their own people. Three of your schoolmates did this last night. Tomorrow they will face the firing squad. The same thing will happen to you if you play with *terroristes*."

Without a word or a glance at the two officers, Robert and his schoolmate left the house. Armed *Miliciens* surrounded the school. The boys crossed to the schoolhouse and paused. A guard stationed at the entry nodded his head, permitting the boys to enter. The teacher was alone at his desk. All the other students had left.

"School has closed for the rest of the term," the teacher said. To the younger boy, he said, "Go home immediately." The boy picked up his books, said *"Ciao"* to Robert, and left quickly.

The teacher then put his hand on Robert's shoulder. "Do not return home!" he whispered urgently. "You must hide. You are sixteen now, and your name will be on the list for the STO.[2] Go out the back door and hide in the woods till dark. Then go immediately to this address in Voiron."

He handed Robert a slip of crumpled paper on which a name and address were written. "If you get caught, chew this paper and swallow it," the teacher said.

Waiting for a chance to leave without being noticed, Robert crouched in the weeds outside the school and eventually made his way downhill into the woods, where he lay down to wait for dark.

He realized now that his teacher worked for the Resistance. He hoped

2 STO (*Service du Travail Obligatoire*): Compulsory labor service for young French men born between 1920-1922 to supply workers for German factories.

the *Milice* didn't suspect the man.

At 10:30 p.m., Robert set off downhill to Voiron, arriving several hours later at the home of Monsieur André, the owner of a small grocery store. "Come down to the cave right away," he told Robert, leading him to the wine cellar. "It's safe down here."

Filling a hungry Robert with potato and cabbage soup—the typical French wartime meal—Monsieur André laid out a pad and blanket, telling him, "You must spend the night and leave early in the morning."

Unbeknownst to Robert, the news of the massacre in Voiron appeared on the front page of the Grenoble newspaper the following day. The funeral services for the Jourdans were followed by arrests, searches, and executions by the *Milice* and Nazis stationed in the region, dividing the population with hatred, sorrow and fear. Several days later, Robert's friend Colonna and two other boys who were Resistance sympathizers were hung and shot in front of their classmates who had been summoned to witness the executions.

With his belly full for the first time in days, and a new address in his pocket, Robert set off in the meantime toward his next destination—the cottage of two elderly widows who lived six miles east of Voiron. Delighted to host the young man, the two women treated him like a son, regaling him with treats from their secret larder. When word came two days later that he was to move again, they hugged him with tears streaming down their faces. They had hidden others who were on the run, but none as young and as sweet as Robert.

On this stretch, Robert had a guide. His instructions were that he was to join a branch of the *Maquis* encamped in the rugged Massif de la Chartreuse, at an elevation of some 5,000 feet. As Robert and the guide began their climb up the steep limestone slopes, the paths grew narrower and narrower. Each step was agony for Robert who lacked the proper footwear for such terrain. But as before, when the *Milice* officer had whipped him, he refused to let out a sound.

It was nightfall when he and the guide reached the plateau of the massif—a cirque at an elevation of about 4000 feet. "This is where we wait," the guide said.

At midnight, the sound of footsteps and a quick flash of light signaled the arrival of their contact. Robert was surprised to see a white-haired man appear. The *maquisard* was equally surprised to see Robert. "*Mon dieu, ils m'ont emmené un poupard,*" the man exclaimed. ("My heavens, they sent me a babe in arms!")

Issued with warm clothing and boots, Robert became a "two-legged mule" for the *Maquis* in the small village of Saint-Même, five miles northeast of the Carthusian Monastery where the monks make their famous green Chartreuse liqueur. Too young at the time for authorization to carry a gun, Robert worked day and night hauling ammunition parachuted to the *Maquis* by the Allies. He learned the routes well and became one of their best workers. "*We had to carry equipment that weighed 50 kilos* (110 lbs.) *or more,*" Robert told me. "*It was back-breaking work, but we had to do it. We had no choice. We just didn't have enough personnel.*"

Since the beginning of that year, Allied bombardments over the region had intensified. Their objectives—to cut rail lines, bomb railroad stations and marshaling yards, blow up roads and German landing fields—were successful in causing damage, but the local French populations suffered greatly, too. On May 26, 1944, just four weeks after Robert's arrival on the Chartreuse plateau, the deafening sound of 65 American Liberator planes resounded over Grenoble. One hundred and fifty-nine tons of bombs rained down on the city in the space of four minutes, causing many deaths in the city and avalanches on the nearby slopes.

In July, the Germans, who had been on the defensive since D-Day but still believed they had the upper hand, began an attack on the *maquisards* of the Vercors, an area in the mountains to the north of the Chartreuse. The Vercors group was larger than Robert's, and over 600 lost their lives in this assault, as did 200 civilians.[3]

On August 13, 1944, the Germans bombed the armory in Saint-Même, but Robert and his small group managed to escape. Ten days later, the American Army liberated Grenoble. Robert returned home to his family, then immediately signed up for the French army. In November, he was sent to the front in Alsace to continue the fight. He was wounded, spent several months recovering, and then rejoined his unit in Innsbruck, Austria, where the Nazis still held the city.

3 *Vercors, 1944, Resistance in the French Alps,* Peter Lieb, Osprey Publishing, 2012.

Following the capitulation of the Germans on May 8, 1945, the new French government called for volunteers to fight in Indochina. Robert declined the "invitation."

"Three of my friends signed up to go," he said. *"Just one came home."* Luck, it seemed, was with Robert all the way.

He spent his last military assignment before being demobilized as part of a quartermaster battalion—a training that led to his future career as a salesman for a prominent grocery chain. He also became a keen cyclist after the war and he met his future wife, Huguette Jouvent, on a bicycling trip to the alpine resort of Chamonix. Eight years later, my trunk and I would arrive at Grenoble's newly rebuilt train station, and Huguette would become one of my adopted French "sisters." However, in 1953 I knew

nothing of the Alpine Resistance movements, nor of the terrible tragedies that had taken place just miles from the house where I was to live, nor at that time would Robert have been willing to tell me of his wartime experiences. The memories were still too raw.

Robert in French army uniform, age 18.

"LES MILICIENS"

A SONG SUNG BY THE FRENCH MAQUIS AND PARTISANS DURING THE WAR

Les Miliciens qui sont Nazis	The Miliciens who are Nazis
Ils les font gardent	They'd better beware
Ils les font gardent	They'd better beware
Les Miliciens qui sont Nazis	The Miliciens who are Nazis
Sont pas aimés dans tout le pays	Are not liked throughout the land
Au marché noir ils ont saisi	On the black market they stole
La boustifaille	The grub
La boustifaille	The grub
Au marché noir ils ont saisi	On the black market they stole
Mais c'est pour leurs petits amis	But it's for their little friends
Miliciens, vous avez trahi	Miliciens, you are traitors
Prenez bien garde	Watch out
Prenez bien garde	Watch out
Miliciens, vous avez trahi	Miliciens, you are traitors
Prenez garde à vos abattis.	Watch out for your guts!

CHAPTER 12

"DON'T COME HOME!"
MARITÉ LE MEUR

One evening in the summer of 2009 Don and I were visiting my French "brother," Geo Jouvent and his wife, Marie-Thérèse (Marité) Le Meur, in Plouha. We were discussing her family's experiences during World War II. Marité was a first cousin to Mimi Gicquel, of the Maison d'Alphonse, *but had not been involved in— or, indeed, aware of—any of the Shelburne Operations, in part because she had been too young at the time. She had a story of her own to tell, however. Raising her leg, she pointed to an indentation in her calf: "Tu vois ce trou?" I ran my finger along the muscle and felt what she referred to as "this hole." She then began to recount the story told here. Though I had known Marité for over 30 years, it was the first time I had ever heard her account.*

Throughout the winter and spring of 1944, fishing along the coasts of France had been banned and mining of French Atlantic beaches had increased. Supported by the Vichy government, the German Military had issued summons for all French men, particularly Breton farmers, to report to centers of defense. Although the BBC had been broadcasting warnings to citizens of Paris and the Atlantic coast to evacuate their towns, fueling the rumors of an Allied invasion, no one in France knew what would happen. Certainly, the Allies were making progress. The Red Army had turned the tide of the war in Russia. Italy had capitulated and Mussolini had been hanged. The new Italian government had declared war on

Germany, and Allied bombings had increased along the entire Atlantic Coast of France.

Along the Côte d'Armor in Brittany, from St. Brieuc to Paimpol, break-ins and robberies at gunpoint committed by hooded *terroristes* were reported daily to the police. Most of these crimes seemed to focus on money and cigarettes, but in reprisal the Gestapo executed, on the spot, any young man caught in the act, or they incarcerated and tortured anyone suspected of being a perpetrator. Female *terroristes* were raped; farms were burned and livestock confiscated. Interrogations increased and no one knew when a dreaded knock on the door might come.

In Plouha, 16-year-old Marité Le Meur was at the end of her spring break in April 1944, packing to return to her Catholic boarding school in Douarnenez. This was the port town on the west coast of Brittany that had served as Gordon Carter's departure point from France in the *Dalc'h Mad* (described in Chapter 9), and for Marité it was a full day's train ride from her home.

Marité's mother, Marie Le Meur, was a widow who supported her two sons and daughter by running a small *café-épicerie* (cafe/grocery) out of their house. Her Icelandic fisherman-husband, André, had died in

The Le Meur house & café.

1939, but Madame Le Meur had been accustomed to his long absences at sea, and she was quite adept at managing the shop and household on her own. The Le Meur's large two-story stone house lay just north of the Saint Samson chapel, a half-mile from the Gicquel's cottage. The ground floor was devoted to the business, with the living quarters above. On farmland adjacent to the house, Madame Le Meur raised chickens and cows and grew vegetables to provide food for the family and the café. During the war years, she served both French and German clientele who came to drink cider or beer (when available) and to play *boules* (a bowling game with steel balls) on the small dirt court behind the house. However, because of the growing tensions along the coast in the early months of 1944, she had reduced her business hours and kept her animals locked up at all times.

Before accompanying her daughter to the bus station that April morning, Madame Le Meur put her hands on Marité's shoulders and said, "Listen to me carefully. If anything should happen that would close your school before the term ends, you must not come home." Her manner was unusually stern: "Look me in the eye, so I know you're paying attention." When Marité raised her head, her mother repeated, "You must not come home. Go with one of your friends, or ask the nuns to find you a safe place. Remain there until you're told it's safe to come home. Do you understand?"

Marité nodded. Madame Le Meur repeated her warning a third time as her daughter stepped onto the bus.

"Yes, Mother, I understand."

Two months later, before dawn on Tuesday, June 6, 1944, Allied troops swarmed ashore on the beaches of Normandy. The D-Day invasion (*Le Débarquement*) had begun.

Throughout France, anyone who tuned to the forbidden midnight broadcasts of the BBC knew something big was about to occur. Coastal inhabitants had been warned to stay at home with everything locked. Everyone hoped this warning was the answer to their questions: "When will the Allies act? When will we be liberated?"

In Douarnenez that morning, the girls at Marité's school had said their morning prayers. Classes were about to begin when word passed from the head nun to the teachers, "School must close now. Send the girls home immediately."

The girls scattered and the school emptied quickly. Everybody was used to these evacuations, as bombings occurred frequently along the coast around Brest. No one paid any attention to Marité, and she didn't say anything to the nuns or other teachers; she was shy and everyone seemed preoccupied. Ignoring her mother's admonition, she decided to return home. She stuffed her few belongings in her small suitcase, filled her knapsack with her books and headed to the train station, running as fast as she could to catch the morning train to Brest. From Brest, she would transfer to the train for Guingamp, and from there she would board the bus to Plouha. She had just enough money for the tickets.

She arrived in Brest at 11:30 a.m. Explosions rocked the city and acrid odors filled the air, worse than Marité had ever experienced before. Fear showed on the faces of the people waiting on the station platform. Her mother's words played round and round in her brain.

An hour later, she boarded the train for Guingamp. It was usually scheduled to continue on to Paris, but on this day no trains would get past Guingamp. None of the passengers were aware of this, as no one

The worst conditions Marité had ever seen.

knew of the orders that had been issued to Allied pilots: *Halt German reinforcements. Target anything moving on rails or roads.*

On board the train were people fleeing Brest. They had baskets, suitcases, pets in their arms. Marité found no place to sit. Passengers crushed against one another, the corridors were jammed. The odor of unwashed bodies and garlic permeated the air. Pressed against a smudgy window, with no place to turn and no fresh air, Marité felt queasy.

From Brest, the railroad curved northeast to Morlaix. The train stopped there briefly, allowing more passengers to squeeze in. It resumed its journey but then, east of Morlaix, on a long, straight stretch of track before the next stop at Plouaret, the train began to slow. Marité heard the screeching of the wheels braking along the tracks, the roar of an airplane, and a barrage of shells hitting the roof. The train stopped. The noise and shelling continued. A conductor ran through the carriages yelling for everyone to get off. *"Tout le monde descend! Tout le monde descend!"*

The passengers pushed and shoved one another, leapt off the train onto the dirt, tripped, fell, scrambled up or downhill, screamed, cried, shouted, moaned. Overhead, an Allied P-51 strafed the tracks, carriages, and surrounding terrain with bullets, hitting passengers indiscriminately, killing some, wounding others.

Dropping down from the right side of her carriage, Marité headed up an incline covered with thick brush and thorns that scratched her bare legs. "If I can just make it to those trees," she thought, "I can hide."

But, halfway up the incline, she was hit by a bullet. She collapsed and fell to the ground. A young man running behind her flung himself over her body as the strafing continued. Fearing another round of shelling, he continued to lie there, not daring to move.

"Can you hear me?" he asked Marité. She did not respond, but he could tell she was still breathing.

The P-51 pulled up, lifted a wing, did a 180°-turn, and swept over the train, strafing once more. When, the plane finally disappeared into the distance, the young man picked Marité up and carried her to a nearby farmhouse. The farmer and his wife laid her on a bed. She was unconscious, and her left calf was bleeding and swollen. She needed a doctor.

"I'll run into the village and see if the doctor can come," the farmer's wife said. The young man remained with Marité, gently stroking her hand, assuring her she would be all right. Eventually the wife returned, bringing the local doctor with her.

As the doctor bent over her, palpating her calf gently but firmly, Marité began to regain consciousness. She was groggy and in pain, not understanding what had happened.

"Young lady," the doctor told her, "this young man brought you here to this farmhouse just in time. Your leg has been penetrated by a bullet. It went straight through your leg, between the muscle and the bone, and came out the other side. You are in luck," he added, explaining that she must have been hit by a tracer bullet, because it had cauterized her wound. "I will not be able to give you any antiseptic or painkillers. The Germans have confiscated all my supplies. Everything. You'll be fine after the wound heals, but you may have a hole in your leg for the rest of your life."

As the farmer's wife tore strips of clean dishtowels to wrap Marité's leg, the young man said good-bye to Marité and set off on foot for a seven-mile hike to his home in Guingamp. Though she would never see him again, tears rolled down her face. She owed her life to him.

She was also, she realized, 25 miles (40 km) from home, without a way to notify her mother or brothers of her whereabouts. She had no idea what to do. The farmer offered to find someone with a truck who could drive her the rest of the way to Plouha. This might be difficult, however, since fuel was tightly rationed and few people could obtain permits. Nor was she in any condition to move. Before he left her, the doctor warned Marité she must not try walking until the swelling diminished and the wound had closed.

She remained at the farmhouse for the next several days. Then early one morning a man in blue overalls showed up with a truck. "I'll take you to Plouha," he said in a surly tone of voice. "But your mother will have to pay me for the fuel. Remember that."

The farmer and the driver carried Marité outside, laid her on straw in the bed of the truck, and the driver set out for Plouha. It was a bumpy, slow, uncomfortable ride. With every bump, Marité moaned with pain.

Four hours later the truck passed the *Maison d'Alphonse* and the Saint Samson Chapel, then pulled up in front of the Le Meur café. The windows were shuttered. The café tables and chairs had been removed from the outside. The house looked abandoned.

The driver got out, went to the front door and pounded it. "Open up! Open up!"

The door opened slightly and Madame Le Meur's face appeared. "What do you want? Everything is closed today."

"I have your daughter," the driver told her gruffly. "Come and get her."

"What are you talking about? My daughter is away."

"No, Madame, she's not . . . she's over there," the driver said, pointing to his truck.

"No! No! How can that be?" Flushed with anger, Madame Le Meur stormed out of the house. "Is that you, Marité?" she shouted. "You disobeyed me! What have you done? Why have you come home? I told you to stay. . ." Then she stopped abruptly, seeing that Marité couldn't move.

Her voice softened. "Oh no. Oh no. What happened? Are you all right?"

"Madame," the driver said impatiently, "Your daughter is wounded and I must leave before curfew, and I need money for my fuel."

"Well, then, help me move my daughter to the house."

Reluctantly, the man carried Marité into the house and upstairs, where he laid her on the couch. Madame Le Meur paid him some money. He then stalked out without an *adieu* or a kind word.

Marité recounted her story, showing her bandaged leg. Her mother hugged her and apologized.

"I was afraid of this happening. That's why I told you to remain in Douarnenez, and not to come home. But now, I'm happy that you're here where I can care for you."

She explained to Marité that the Allies had landed in Normandy and that battles were in full force along the northern parts of the French coast. People hoped to be liberated soon, but the Germans and White Russians conscripts had increased all of their coastal patrols in the meantime and everyone was nervous and frightened. "We have to stay inside. I only go out to the barn to tend to the cows and chickens," she said. "We've been warned not to go anywhere unless it's an emergency."

Marité's condition was an emergency, but the Germans had cut off telephone service to the entire coastal zone. The next morning, Madame

Le Meur hiked into Plouha to find the doctor, who agreed to come immediately. Medical doctors had permits for their own automobiles, so the doctor was able to drive Madame Le Meur back to her house with him.

Examining Marité, the doctor told Madame Le Meur, "The doctor who attended your daughter at the farmhouse made the correct assessment. The tracer bullet cauterized her wound. I can only dress it with clean bandages and remind you that you must not let her walk until I give permission."

Within a month, Marité was able to walk again. In the meantime, each evening, at curfew, the Le Meur house was shuttered and locked. And, before midnight, Marité, her mother and her brothers would head upstairs to the attic, turn on the radio and listen to the BBC.

They would learn that the Allied troops were gaining ground, week by week. The cities of Brest, Lorient, and St. Nazaire along Brittany's Atlantic Coast—each with German submarine bases—had been devastated by the Allied bombings. Perhaps the BBC could tell them what the smaller towns along the Côte d'Armor could expect?

In Plouha, one response to the Allied invasion had been the takeover

German and Russian Conscripts fleeing the Americans.

of the local Army post by the Gestapo. Another was that both German officers and local people stopped frequenting the Le Meur Café.

On July 24, around four o'clock in the afternoon, the sound of explosions reverberated throughout Plouha. Marité and her mother peered out the door. They saw to their horror a billowing cloud of black smoke rising at the end of the road, the odor of the smoke permeating the air. "Oh no! That's Mimi's house," said Madame Le Meur.

Later that evening, the Le Meurs would learn that the *Maison d'Alphonse* had been set on fire by the Germans, and that their Gicquel cousins—Mimi, Jean and their baby girl—had escaped and were in hiding. That same night Jean Gicquel was safely evacuated to England by MGB 502, along with the SAS men, in the second *Opération Crozier* described in Chapter 8.

Germans swarmed through the area in the days that followed, fleeing eastwards in the hope of avoiding capture by the Americans. Plouha was liberated on August 6, 1944, two months after the Normandy landings, and Marité stayed on in the village, completing her education at home with her family and friends nearby.

After the war, Marité married my French "brother" from Grenoble, Geo Jouvent. The couple lived and worked in Paris, but Marité inherited the family house in Plouha after her mother's death and the Jouvents spent their summers there. In numerous visits to Geo and Marité, Don and I came to know Plouha and to learn its stories.

The Le Meur-Jouvent family, 1956. Marité has her arm around her mother, Marie. Geo Jouvent is at Marité's right. In front are the couple's two daughters, Pascale (right) and Sylvie (left).

Geo and Marité, 1956

Marité (at right) with her cousin Mimi Gicquel (of the Maison d'Alphonse), 2010.

In May 2010, Marité died suddenly and unexpectedly. My kind, talented and gentle friend will live always in my memory.

Kenavo,[1] Marité. Tu vivras toujours dans ma mémoire.

---

1 *Kenavo*: Breton for *au revoir*.

B-24 pilot Ken Sorgenfrei with his crew.
L to R, top row: Ken Sorgenfrei, Ray Swedzinsky,
Joe Bonzek, Carl Pacharzina.
Bottom: Bill Hensley, Ted Turbak, Marvin Wycoff, Paul
Petersen, Edwin Mandlavitz, Stanley Radzewski.

CHAPTER 13

MISSION 44
KEN SORGENFREI

Several years ago, after I had started work on this book, an aviator friend of ours who had retired from a commercial airline told us we should meet one of his fellow pilots, Ken Sorgenfrei. Our friend had served as his airline co-pilot and "Sorgey" had told him numerous stories about his experiences as a B-24 pilot in WWII and being saved by the French Resistance after his plane was shot down just before the liberation of France. Sorgey lives within a few hours' drive of our home in Washington State, so in July 2012 I made contact with him and spent an afternoon interviewing him at his home in the Cascade foothills, above Seattle. Sorgey is a delightful man, and his experiences on the ground in France were of particular interest to me because his plane had come down near Grenoble. He gave me several boxfuls of information after our interview, as well as a copy of a published French account of his story, Onze Américains Tombés du Ciel [*Eleven Americans Fell from the Sky*], *by Pierre Montaz. Thereafter, I contacted Montaz, who gave me permission to use images and excerpts from his book. Sorgey's story, as presented here, is a compilation of information presented in* Onze Américains, *Sorgey's personal files, and my own interview notes.*

Sorgey's story began on March 23, 1944, when he and his crew of nine climbed into a brand new B-24 bomber in Topeka, Kansas, and flew it to Spinazzolla, in southeastern Italy. The bombers had been delivered to Kansas from a Boeing plant in Michigan by female (WASP) pilots. Sorgey and his crew took a further 19 days to fly the plane the 5,900 nautical miles to their assigned base in Italy, with seven fuel stops along the way.[1]

As the B-24's pilot, Ken Sorgenfrei was a 21-year-old USAAF First Lieutenant with only 250 hours flying time under his belt. At the outset of the war, USAAF pilots trained for two years. As the conflict progressed, and more and more pilots were lost, the training period became both shorter and more intensive and demanding. Sorgey and his crew had gone through highly accelerated training in just six months. This began with psychological tests to determine character, temperament and physical endurance, followed by three months of theory and practice in Wyoming, New Mexico, and Texas. The men were together from the outset, so knew one another well and worked as a disciplined, tightly-knit squad. They were a proud mix of American polyglot heritage and religion: Swedish, Polish, Norwegian; Catholic, Protestant, Jewish, with a tongue-in-cheek motto, "The Pure Americans."

Their four-engine B-24 J was a hulking vessel, unattractive but reliable. Sorgey's co-pilot, Ray Swedzinsky, said "It flew well, was easy to handle and tolerated a lot of shells." The interior, as on all B-24s, was unfinished. Wires, cables, and ducts criss-crossed the inside of the fuselage. There was no heating and no sound-proofing. To withstand the freezing high-altitude temperatures of the bombing runs—minus 30°F (-35°C) to minus 40°F (-40°C)—and the lack of oxygen at higher altitudes, the crew wore heavy leather jackets lined with lambs wool, insulated pants, heavy flight boots, and oxygen masks.

After their arrival in Italy in mid-April 1944, Sorgey and his crew flew some 43 bombing missions in the next three months—a schedule even more grueling than their training. They had several close calls while bombing industrial targets over Germany, with their original plane so badly damaged that it had to be scrapped. Even so, the bombing runs had become "old hat" and, after their 44th mission, their tour of duty would be over and they would go home.

Their last mission was scheduled for July 19. Thirty planes would go out; their target was the rail yards of Munich. The challenges would be

---

1 West Palm Beach, Florida; Trinidad; Belem, Brazil; Fortaleza, Brazil; Dakar, Senegal; Marrakech, Morocco; and Tunis, Tunisia. Pierre Montaz, *Onze Aviateurs Tombés du Ciel*, p. 21.

Members of Ken Sorgenfrei's crew, dressed for temperatures below -30°F. From left: Radziewski, Petersen, Turbak.

the same as always: navigating through the thick black smoke of anti-aircraft fire to locate their objective, releasing their half-ton bombs, then hightailing it back over the Alps to safety in Italy. Sorgey's plane took off with its usual 10-man complement, plus an extra man, Technical Sergeant Mike Bisek, a combat photographer who had such faith in Ken Sorgenfrei's reputation that he asked to be transferred from another plane.

As they reached their destination and released their bombs over the rail yards, a furious barrage of German anti-aircraft guns struck their group. Sorgey watched two of their squadron planes spin out of control down to the ground. A third exploded in the air with no time for any of the crew to bail out.

Then, Sorgey's own plane took a major hit. The nose turret was blown off; two out of four engines were dead; the electrical circuits and oxygen supply were cut. *We'll never make it home to Italy,* thought Sorgenfrei. "Plot a course for Switzerland," he instructed his navigator, Carl Pacharzina. "At least we'll land in neutral territory."

"Lighten the load!" he shouted to the rest of his crew. Second Lieutenant Joe Bonzek, the bombardier, immediately released the remainder of their bombs. The other men tossed out machine guns, ammunition, anything that would lighten the load for a likely crash landing.

They had abandoned the formation group, and with two engines out

157

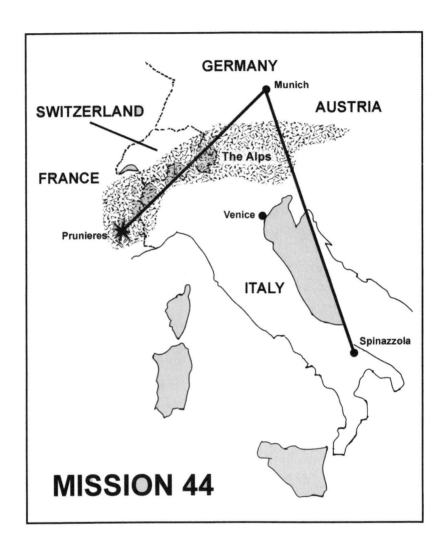

of action the plane began to lose altitude. As long as the two remaining engines continued to function, they had some hope of finding a landing site. But an hour later a third engine quit and the navigation equipment failed. The plane was done for. Sorgey gave the order: *"Everyone out!"*

He recalled the moments that followed as being dreamlike. He remembered giving the order, and remembered telling his co-pilot, Ray Swedzinsky, to bail out. Then, as the last one to bail out, he found himself floating in the air, with the sound of his plane above him. He heard the plane crash and explode—and then he lost consciousness.

When Sorgey awoke, he found himself in a farmhouse, in a soft bed with a woman leaning over him, trying to feed him goat's milk. The taste was repulsive and he immediately vomited.

He and his crew had unknowingly overflown Switzerland and had exited their plane over southeastern France. Sorgenfrei had been knocked out as he parachuted into a small valley near the alpine village of Prunières, about 50 miles south of Grenoble, in German-occupied territory. The other ten men had landed safely nearby. Ted Turbak, rear gunner, had landed in a potato field. A person immediately headed toward him, Ted put his hands up to surrender, thinking it would be a German. But "the person" happened to be a 14-year old French girl who greeted him first, in French, saying "We are neither Germans, nor collaborators." Then seeing that Ted did not understand French, she said "I love you"— the only English she knew.

As the rest of the crew scrambled out of their flying gear, local villagers appeared on the scene to help them bury their parachutes, then hurry them into the safety of the surrounding mountains.

The sound of the crash had reverberated around the entire area and smoke billowed from the wreck of the plane. Both caught the attention of the German troops billeted at a garrison a few miles away. When the Germans arrived at the site in armored cars, they were furious to find no sign of survivors or bodies. After pumping machine gun rounds into the plane, they stormed into the village looking for Americans.

Sorgenfrei was in rough shape. On landing, the skin on one side of his face had been badly scraped off. He had a seriously sprained ankle and a concussion that was to leave him with double vision for months afterwards.

In spite of this, the local Resistance members had no choice but to take him into the hills to join the rest of his crew. As he left the farmhouse, he unpinned his military wings and gave them to the farmer's wife.

In the mountains, Sorgenfrei tried to convince the Resistance members to take him and his crew to Switzerland. "The *maquisards* were a ragtag group, unshaven, disorganized, undisciplined and without hierarchy," he recalled. "They had no way to take care of us. They had no supplies, no food, especially for a group of hungry American fliers." He asked them if they could hand him and his crew over to another group of *maquisards* capable of leading them over the mountains.

Over the course of the next few days the eleven men fled from village to village, always moving higher into mountains. In one village, they met an American Captain—apparently a Resistance organizer. The Captain was strangely cool in his manner towards them and refused to help. To this day, French people who were in the area insist there never was such an American. "But we know he was there," Sorgenfrei said. "We saw him. I believe he was a secret operative of some kind."[2]

While the *maquisards* carried weapons, Sorgenfrei's band of Americans travelled without them. Ironically, this was for their own safety. If they were caught with guns, they would be considered *terroristes* and shot on sight. If caught unarmed, rules of engagement were supposed to apply and they could be taken only as Prisoners of War. Either way, the chances of capture remained high. "There was a price on our heads, and there was a price on the heads of every one of the *maquisards*," Sorgenfrei said. He added that, "If the Germans caught the *maquisards*, they'd be tortured and executed." However, compliance with such orders depended on the German officer in charge and, as the war turned against Germany, the rules were often hardened.

The eleven Americans traveled on through the Alps and were finally turned over to Resistance members of l'Oisans. The Resistance fighters in this region were under the command of Alfred Lanvin, who would later serve in the French conflicts in Vietnam, and Noël Monod, a Parisian who served after the War as a treasurer of the United Nations. The goal of their group was to defend a mountain pass against the 10,000 German troops

---

2 During this phase of the war secret American operatives, who were sworn to secrecy, were being dropped in various areas of France to direct and aid organized Resistance groups.

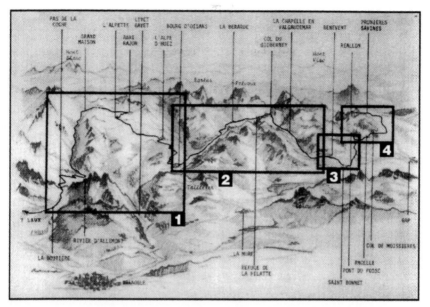

Area 1: With the Maquis d'Oisons, Le Bourg d'Oisons
Area 2: With Jeunesse et Montagne, St. Bonnet - Le Bourg d'Oisons
Area 3: Americans left to themselves to try to make it to Switzerland
Area 4: With the High Alpine Resistance

*The escape route followed by Sorgenfrei and
his companions in the mountains.*

Makeshift Maquis *'hospital'.*

in the region.

The airmen were taken to an abandoned ski resort, l'Alpe d'Huez, at 6,069 feet elevation (1,850 meters). The site was used as a hideaway for occasional night raids—blowing up bridges, railways and highways— and also as a field hospital for wounded Resistance fighters. Two chalets with a maximum of 30 beds, a poorly equipped "operating room" and few medical supplies had been set up a few days earlier, after being moved up from a previous, less safe location at a lower elevation. The operating room comprised little more than a table and a light from an automobile refashioned by 19 year-old Resistance member, Pierre Montaz. Montaz also manufactured "orthopedic devices" from scrap metal. A pressure cooker was used to sterilize instruments, which the surgeon, Dr. Tisserand, had bought from a retreating Italian medical officer in 1943. Dr. Tisserand also possessed a microscope, and despite the lack of medical supplies, anesthesia, and anti-tetanus and anti-gangrene serums, not one of the surgical patients in the makeshift hospital succumbed to infection.

Local villagers were compelled to share their meager food allowance with the rescued men and the *maquisards*, most of whom had no ration cards. Pierre Montaz later wrote that "everything was exchanged, everything was stolen. Hunger makes everyone desperate."

The Americans were not allowed to join in the guerrilla warfare but they could help care for the half-dozen wounded guerrillas being treated there. They worked at the hospital for nearly two weeks. Conditions were miserable. Doctors amputated the legs of two men without anesthesia; Sorgenfrei helped hold one of them down during the operation. One of the patients, who had been shot in the head by German troops, survived being tossed into a river and a three-mile float before being pulled out of the water by Resistance members.

About ten days after the Americans arrived at l'Alpe d'Huez, the Germans learned of the mountain hideout. Resistance members believed the nurse in their midst had betrayed them and they killed her. Using mules, donkeys and carts from nearby farms, they then quickly packed up the hospital to move higher into the mountains. They were a motley crew of about twenty—the eleven airmen, two doctors, a half-dozen patients, the wife of one of the doctors and the fiancée of one of the wounded resistance members. Two of the patients had no legs, one was blind, the doctor's wife was eight and a half months pregnant, and Sorgenfrei was still suffering from double vision.

For the next three days the wagon train made its way up the mountainside, with the Germans in pursuit. As the terrain became too steep for the animals and farm carts, the Germans began to close the gap. Bullets ricocheted as the Americans took turns carrying the wounded on stretchers. By this time, they had reached an elevation of 12,000 feet (3,657 meters). Rocky slopes gave way to rocky cliffs. The wounded men, the pregnant woman, and one other member of the party were unable to climb the cliffs and had to be left behind, hidden in a rock cleft. Sorgenfrei and the others helped pile rocks around them to conceal their location from the Germans. They then watched as some forty German troops swarmed across the meadow toward them, appearing as a sea of gray-green uniforms.

The French members of the group split away from the Americans and began shooting haphazardly. "At first I thought they were the wildest shots I'd ever seen," said Sorgenfrei. "Then I realized they were trying to distract the Germans so we could get away."

None of the Americans were hurt in the skirmish and they spent the next few days on the mountain with little food and no shelter. The nights were cold. The men could hear anti-artillery fire coming from Grenoble, which lay below them.

On August 22, a month after Sorgenfrei and his crew crash-landed their plane, Allied forces liberated Grenoble. A week later, the airmen walked down off the mountain into the liberated city. For them, the war was over. They were paraded through Grenoble as heroes. Women wore flowers and blouses made of parachute silk—perhaps from the same parachutes Sorgenfrei and his crew had used to float down to earth those long weeks before.

In Grenoble, the airmen learned that the group of wounded they left behind in the rocky mountain shelter had survived. The Germans had come perilously close but had not spotted them, and the group of wounded was later rescued.

By October 1944, Sorgenfrei was on his way home, traveling by hospital ship. He spent months in a veterans' hospital recovering from his injuries, including persistent double vision. The rest of his crew returned to the U.S. separately on a troop ship.

The crew drifted apart and did not see one another again for 38 years, until they were invited to a dedication in France of a mountainside monument to the Resistance members of l'Oisans. Nine of Sorgenfrei's crew attended the ceremony—one had died in a motorcycle accident after the War, and one had not kept in touch. Three years later, in 1985, some of the airmen returned yet again to France and retraced their steps from the valley into which they had crash-landed, up the mountain pass and back down to the valley. The French gave them a reception afterwards and invited villagers to greet them—the same villagers who had found each of them after the crash.

"The little girl who had told Ted Turbak, `I love you,' was there," said Sorgenfrei. "And a woman walked up to me and said, `The last time I saw you, I was in my mother's tummy.' And another woman was wearing my silver wings—it was the woman who had tried to feed me the goat's milk. I couldn't believe they all were there. They were so kind. That's what I remember the most . . . I can't forget their kindness."

In October 2013, when Don and I were in France, I met Pierre Montaz and his wife, Pat, in person, at their home in Savoie. Now 89 years old, Pierre spent his working life designing and building ski lifts in France and around the world. His family home is about three hours' drive from the site where Ken Sorgenfrei's B-24 crashed. Pierre drove me from there up into the French Alps along steep 4WD tracks that followed the route Sorgenfrei and his crew took to l'Alpe d' Huez in 1944. I was amazed at the distances the aviators covered and tried to imagine them struggling up those rugged slopes in their slippery-soled flight boots. The next day I was privileged to attend a commemoration for Sorgenfrei and his crew, which Pierre had arranged in honor of my visit. A crowd of local people looked on as re-enactors, dressed in WWII-era U.S. Army uniforms and French Resistance clothing, marched past bearing flags from our two countries (the U.S. flag contributed by my brother, Brigadier General Thomas L. Hemingway, USAF Ret). In a five-minute speech in French, I spoke about my lifelong relationship with "my second country," the spirit of friendship and co-operation between France and the United States, and how we Americans were proud to have been able to help the French people during the War, as they had helped our airmen, sailors and soldiers. Those of us who knew the words sang The Star Spangled Banner, Le Marseillaise, *and* Chant des Partisans (Song of the Partisans, *the first two stanzas of which are printed below). I found this occasion to be extremely moving, and I feel honored to have been part of it.*

Réanne with Pierre Montaz at the Commemoration for Sorgenfrei.

CHANT DES PARTISANS
(SONG OF THE PARTISANS)

Ami, entends-tu	Friend, do you hear
Le vol noir des corbeaux	The black flight of crows
Sur nos plaines?	Above our plains?
Les cris sourds du pays	The muffled cries of the country
Qu'on enchaîne?	That is in chains?
Ohé! partisans,	Hey, partisans,
Ouvriers et paysans	Workers and peasants,
C'est l'alarme!	This is the alarm!
Ce soir l'ennemi	This evening the enemy
Connaîtra le prix du sang	Will know the price of blood
Et des larmes!	And tears!
Montez de la mine,	Come up from the mine,
Descendez des collines,	Descend the hills,
Camarades!	Comrades!
Sortez de la paille	Take out from the haystacks
Les fusils, la mitraille,	The rifles, machine guns,
Les grenades …	Grenades…
Ohé! les tueurs,	Hey, killers,
A la balle et au couteau,	With the bullet and the knife,
Tuez vite!	Kill quickly!
Ohé! saboteur,	Hey saboteur,
Attention à ton fardeau:	Watch out for your burden:
Dynamite!	Dynamite!

*A squadron of B-17s conducting a daylight
bombing raid over a German target.*

CHAPTER 14

ROUGH LAST DAYS
OVER GERMANY, 1945
WOODY BLONDFIELD

BY DON DOUGLASS

I first met Woody in 1963 when he hired me to work with him as a project engineer at Beckman Instruments in Fullerton, California. He quickly became a trusted mentor at work and a friend who would take me with him on lunchtime flying trips to Catalina Island. We'd land on a little dirt strip and eat barbecued buffalo burgers at a ranch café, then head back to work. On the weekends, Woody and I would fly to Mammoth Lakes, where we'd ski during the day and return to Fullerton at midnight. In 1967, Woody arranged a special flight to Apple Valley, in the San Bernardino foothills, so I could propose marriage to Réanne. This is a memory she and I will never forget. My proposal coincided with an abrupt downdraft as we were flying through Cajon Pass. Woody was busy trying to control the plane, a single-engine Comanche 260. Réanne was nodding her head in response to my popping of the question, while Woody and I thought she was shaking with fright.

Woody quickly became my World War II hero. His accounts of bombing Germany every few nights for months at a time in 1945, and controlling the panic among his crew as they prepared for crash landings, will remain with me always. He also volunteered to drop food behind enemy lines to starving Dutch citizens. Woody set a high standard when it came to caring for others, and his warmth, compassion, bravery and leadership were an inspiration to everyone he met. When Réanne began work on this book I felt his story deserved inclusion. We interviewed him formally over several days at the home he shared with his lovely wife, Bebe, in Apple Valley, California, in 2011.

Elwood (Woody) Blondfield was 21 years old when he received his notice in 1942 to report for the World War II draft. He was a freshman at UCLA majoring in science and his top grades gave him entry to pilot training. By June 1944, he received a commission as Second Lieutenant in the U.S. Army Air Force. Six months later, he became one of 20 elite pilots chosen for a secret assignment to fly new B-17s to England across the North Atlantic for the final push against Berlin. These aircraft had just come off the assembly lines at the Boeing factory in Seattle, Washington, and had been flown by Women Airforce Service Pilots (WASPs) from that city to Nebraska with uncalibrated instruments, a feat that attests to the piloting skills of these women.[1] Woody and other pilots spent the next two weeks calibrating the instruments and test-flying the airplanes in preparation for their overseas assignments, including the bombing raids that would become part of the final Allied push to take Berlin.

In December 1944, Woody landed his new B-17 in England and was assigned to the 350th Squadron of the 100th Bombardment Group (Heavy) at Thorpe Abbotts, an RAF base in Norfolk that had been taken over by the U.S. 8th Air Force. Two months later, on February 20, 1945, he and his crew were dispatched on their first mission, which was to bomb the railroad marshaling yards in Nuremberg.

Their strategy, as for all bombing missions, was to climb as high as possible to reduce the chances of being hit by anti-aircraft fire (flak). The highest altitude they could reach was 30,000 feet, but the bombing runs were usually well below that. Above 12,000 feet, the men all wore oxygen masks. They also wore flak jackets, Mae West life jackets, and "zoot suits" (thin nylon pants and vests) over their flight suits, which were wired for heat and plugged into DC voltage outlets. In the event that they were shot down, their parachute harnesses contained a kit that included a knife, a loaded morphine syringe (in case of injury), some dry food, and a set of

---

1 After the War the WASPS received significant praise for their accomplishments.

remarkable silk maps showing details of the ground they were to fly over. The officers also carried semi-automatic pistols, though Woody professed to be such a bad shot that he would have done more harm by simply throwing his gun. In any case, on that first mission to Nuremberg, it was his superior flight training and skill as a pilot that ultimately came to be tested, rather than his shooting prowess.

The 350th squadron had dropped its load of bombs on the marshaling yards in Nuremburg, and Woody watched as flames and black smoke billowed up from the ground. Then, suddenly, his B-17 was hit and thrown out of formation. "Flak got us. Flak got us," Woody shouted through the intercom to his crew. "Engine Number 2 hit. Number 1 out. Underneath flaps knocked out. Fuel too low. Won't make it back to England." Woody did not order his crew to bail out, however. During their 3:00 a.m. flight briefing at Thorpe Abbotts, the squadron had been given the location of a landing field at Florennes, in Belgium, 60 miles south of Brussels and west of the German-occupied area of the country. This was one of a number of so-called Advanced Landing Grounds that were established behind the Allied front lines to serve as temporary bases for tactical fighter groups supporting the advancing Allied ground armies. The field at Florennes had in fact served the same purpose for the Luftwaffe when the Germans occupied that part of Belgium, but it had been taken over by the Allies in September 1944 and now did double duty as an emergency landing field for damaged Allied bombers.

"I'm going to try to make it," Woody told his engineer, Royal Brooks. "Go back and tell the guys I won't activate the abandon ship bell. I'll try to fly marginally till I find the airstrip and get this 'puppy' landed. If they want to bail out, there won't be any negative criticism if they're caught as POWs."[2]

Woody's North Atlantic crossing had already given him a taste of the dangers ahead of him. Between Labrador and Iceland, the temperature on the oil gauges had peaked on three of the B-17's four engines. Woody had noticed, however, that the temperature of the cylinder heads remained in the green. Disagreeing with his co-pilot's advice to feather the props (i.e,

---

2 Some combat GIs considered aviators who ended in POW camps as cowards who "sat out the war." Other airmen went down with their aircraft or made desperate attempts at evasion. Debate continues among historians and war veterans alike as to which response was "best."

turn them parallel to the oncoming wind to reduce drag), which would slow the plane, Woody continued to Reykjavik, Iceland, at normal speed, knowing from his Arctic survival training that if he and his crew had to ditch the plane and bail out over the North Atlantic, they'd never survive in the frigid waters. They had really no choice but to keep all engines running.

The weather over Germany reminded Woody of that North Atlantic crossing. Europe was suffering from its severest winter in 50 years and thousands of wounded Allied infantrymen had frozen to death in the Battle of the Ardennes just a few months before. This day, February 20th was freezing, also, and at the altitude Woody's B-17 was flying the outside air temperature was minus -49F (-45°C). Bailing out was not an option.

"If I can just stabilize this plane," Woody thought, "we may be able to reach that emergency airfield."

The flight engineer reported back. "No one's hurt, Woody . . . and to a man, each of the guys says if you're going to try to put this plane in Belgium, they're with you. And so am I."[3]

This only reinforced Woody's determination. He knew his crew to be a great bunch of guys. He owed it to them to make that Belgian airfield. The plane was descending ever more rapidly, however, with the gas tanks leaking and the fuel gauges dropping at an abnormal rate. Eventually Woody managed to stabilize the plane, but it was an effort to keep it flying straight and level, with two engines out and the other two feathered on the same side.

Then came the voice of his navigator, Monty Montagne: "We've crossed over the German lines, Woody. We're out of enemy territory! I figure about 15 more minutes and we should sight the field."

Visibility rapidly decreased. Thick, lowland fog swept the countryside. Woody shouted back to Monty: "It's up to you. Give me the correct bearings and get us lined up to make an approach."

As Monty fed him the information Woody began the descent to locate the field. They should be right on top of it. He made one pass without seeing anything. Then another pass, and another. The fuel gauges now pointed to empty. Woody made one more pass and the fog parted just long enough for him to sight the field. He lined up to make the landing

---

3 As Woody told us this story 65 years later, tears welled up in his eyes.

Woody and crew. Woody is at top left.

and brought the plane down safely. It came to a stop and a loud cheer broke out from Woody's nine crew members.

Their problems weren't quite over, however. The airfield was primitive; their B-17 was beyond repair; and they had no way of communicating with their base in England. After several days of waiting on the ground, Woody decided to examine an old B-24 that sat unused on the landing field. Could they possibly get it started and fly back to home base?

The answer appears in a terse notation in the log of Woody's tail-gunner, Earl Valentine: *Made hectic landing. No gas left. Spent two days in Belgium. Came back to base on an old B-24.*

Woody recalled that he and his crew were considered Missing in Action (MIA) before they made it back to their base in England. Other crews in their squadron had seen their damaged plane disappear into the clouds, with no sign of anyone bailing out. He added that the B-24 wasn't in much better shape than their old B-17, and he had never flown one before. *But you do what you do. You look at the situation and say, "I can do this," and if it works you just keep going.*

Back in England, Woody's fellow pilots looked at him as if to say, "Hey, where'd you come from?" He then had to round up his clothes because, as he explained, *When you're MIA the first thing that happens is the supply officer comes and closes up your foot locker with all your personal stuff in it, puts a steel band around it, and puts it in storage in the supply room. If you never make it back, it gets shipped to your family as remains.*

Woody and his crew resumed flying from Thorpe Abbotts with the 350th Squadron in a new B-17, nicknamed the "Heaven Sent." In the next month they flew ten more bombing missions over Germany. Their targets included the shipyards at Bremen; rail marshaling yards at Kassel, Dortmund and Hanover; steel works at Brunswick; oil refineries at Seguien and Hamburg; jet factories at Frankfurt; and the Zeiss Optical Works at Jena. On one return trip to Thorpe Abbotts, Earl Valentine's log read: *Saw ruins of Cologne, Koblenz and other cities on the Rhine.*

The 350th Squadron had been fortunate up to this time—they hadn't lost any men. Its parent 100th Bomb Group had not been so lucky, however. Early on, it had earned its name, "The Bloody 100th" for the heavy losses it had incurred. These continued in the months that followed. The combined Heavy Bomb Groups of the 8th Air Force Bomber Command ultimately lost 27,000 airmen killed in action, with 44,000 total casualties—more losses than were incurred by the Marines in WWII Pacific operations.

Additional losses were incurred through stress, though some men recovered sufficiently to be able to return to duty. Woody worked with one fellow B-17 pilot who suffered a complete nervous breakdown after returning from a mission in which an 88mm flak shell came up through the floor of his cockpit, split open one of his shoes and the leg of his pants, and continued on up through the roof. The pilot flew the plane back and landed it successfully, but then he collapsed as soon as his feet hit the tarmac. *These things go on in your mind,* Woody said, *and you don't really understand it until you've finished. Your nerves can be shattered and you're not even aware of it.*

The pilot spent two weeks in the hospital, during which time the flight surgeon concluded the only way the man would recover was to get him flying again. Woody agreed to help and spent the next few weeks, when he wasn't flying missions, taking the pilot up on calm days, initially as a passenger and then gradually re-introducing him to the techniques

The 'Heaven Sent.'

of flying: *First time up, I put him in the right seat and just let him sit there. Then I started banking, diving, putting him through that. The next flight, I said, "I want you to put your hands on the wheel. I want you to touch vertical. That's all we're going to do." When we got to where he was relaxed with this, I said, "Now I want you to put your feet on the rudder pedals." The flight after that, I said, "I want you to fly this airplane."* After about six flights Woody switched the man over to the pilot's seat, and within a month his friend was ready to fly missions again.

On March 21, 1945, Woody and his crew set out on their twelfth mission, little knowing they were about to face their own ultimate test. Their orders for the day were to bomb a tank factory at Plauen, in east-central Germany near the Czech border. This was 600 miles from Thorpe Abbotts Base, the maximum range of the B-17. The men reported to the briefing room at 0300 hours and took off before dawn for their long day's journey.

Anti-aircraft artillery (flak) had caused the most casualties among the 350th Squadron's planes to date, and had brought down Woody's original B-17, among many others. But on this day, the squadron had their first encounter with the formidable Luftwaffe Messerschmitt Me 262 fighter jet.

The Me 262 had undergone a lengthy and controversial trial period and the Germans had delayed putting it into service. By mid-1944, the planes had finally begun coming off the assembly lines and the training of pilots commenced. The jets could attain speeds of up to 540 mph and climb almost 4,000 feet per minute, far outperforming Allied fighter planes and exceeding the airspeed of B-17 bombers by 150 mph or more. They were also highly maneuverable. According to ace Luftwaffe pilot General Johannes Steinhoffer, if the Me 262 had been available in 1943, with trained pilots and adequate fuel, it might have changed the course of the war.[4]

The first large-scale attack by Me 262 jets against Allied bombers eventually occurred on March 18, 1945. On this occasion, thirty-seven Me 262s intercepted a force of 1,221 bombers and 632 escorting fighters. Twelve bombers and one Allied fighter were shot down, along with three of the Me 262s. For the Allies, the losses were statistically minor. However,

4 Interview with Steinhoffer, from *World War II* magazine, February 2000.

for Woody and his crew, who had their own fateful encounter with the jets a mere three days later, the statistics were irrelevant as their own bomber became one of those hit.

The Me 262 carried twenty-four R4M rockets, in addition to four 30mm cannon. The latter fired cylindrical shells that were six inches long with detonator heads that exploded on contact, allowing the shells to penetrate and blow up under the skin of an airplane. When this occurred, the steel case of the shell broke into hundreds of small knife-like blades that penetrated the interior of the aircraft. The exploding shells were much more lethal than the 50-caliber machine guns carried aboard U.S. aircraft, which fired smaller, non-explosive lead slugs that left a hole the size of a finger and did not always bring down their target.

On March 21st, the 350th Squadron reached Plauen, in eastern Germany, around noon and began dropping their bombs over the tank factory. Woody's plane was second in formation and had just released its load when the Number 2 engine was hit by flak. This was a bad thing to happen such a long way from base, but it was just the beginning of their problems.

Five Me 262s, flying in echelon directly off "Heaven Sent's" tail, began to give chase. The jets entered the squadron's formation from the flank, shooting their rockets from the side, then pulling up and away at full-speed and making a rear pass on any B-17s that had survived the onslaught.

From his position in the tail, gunner Earl Valentine watched as one of the B-17s beside them burst into flames and exploded in mid-air. There was no chance of survivors. Immediately afterward, their own plane took five of the powerful 30mm shells. One exploded between the third and fourth engine, knocking both out of commission. It also blew a large amount of skin away from under the wing area, sucking out the fuel bags and taking out the flaps. The second shell took off the right wing tip. The third shell tore away the flaps between the first and second engine. The fourth took a large chunk off the right horizontal stabilizer. The fifth shell exploded inside the radio room, severing most of the cables in the ceiling of the fuselage that led to the empennage, the tail assembly that stabilizes the airplane and controls direction.

Just one strand of the multi-strand cables to the elevator remained. Those leading to the elevator trim were completely cut. The servomotors in the tail driving the control surfaces to the autopilot were now inoperative.

As the aircraft nosed up and began to spin violently out of control its fate was now solely in the hands of Woody and his co-pilot, James Dizmang.

Woody recalled, *It took both Dizmang and me pushing on the wheel to get the nose down and prevent the spin. We pushed so hard the wheel started to bend over and the bakelite plastic cracked away from its steel-rod core. But we kept pushing and pushing and finally managed to stabilize flight. I knew, though, that I'd never be able to control this unbelievable force for long, and that we'd never make it to an emergency landing field unless we got rid of the weight in the back of the plane.*

Woody directed his flight engineer, Royal Brooks, to go back to assess damages and injuries. Lawrence Hlavka, the radio operator, had been hit by flak in his heel and lower leg, but everyone else on board was uninjured. Woody then ordered them to jettison everything they could. First the starboard waist door, then guns, ammunition, radio amplifiers, servo system, all electronics—anything loose they could get their hands on.

The crew did all of this as I was descending to a lower altitude so we could take off our oxygen masks. I dove through three separate cloud formations to shake off any jet fighters that might have ideas of finishing us off. The last German fighter to fly over our fuselage was so close I could see him looking down at me as if saying, "You're destroyed. How come you're still flying when you're falling apart?"

But, I dodged this jet by diving as steeply as I dared through another cloudbank, hoping he'd keep on his horizontal track and pass us. We lost altitude quickly which, with the weight loss, gave us a smaller gliding circle and, by a long shot, I was able to resume horizontal flight with the two right engines feathered.

The challenge now was to find a place to land once they crossed the German combat zone. With their radio-room gear destroyed or thrown out, they couldn't make contact with anyone on the ground. However, one piece of communications equipment was undamaged—a radio compass receiver located in the cockpit. Woody hoped it might just lead them back to an emergency airfield, like the one in Florennes that had saved them on their first mission.

During his 0300 briefing that morning Woody had once again been given the location of several emergency airfields in Belgium.[5] He also knew that the fields could be located from the air by homing-in on radio beacons that were mounted on a jeep within 5-8 miles of each field. This required that the radio compass be tuned to the frequency of the beacons. Woody and his crew did this, and picked up a signal. But as Woody put it, "just to make things more challenging," the field they were aiming for was buried in the midst of a fog bank several thousand feet thick that spread for a hundred miles in all directions.

We descended into the fog and homed-in on the beacon, took the prescribed heading and flew the plotted distance. But no field. Monty came up to the cockpit, almost crying. "My God, what do we do now? There's no field down there."

"We'll go back to the beacon," I told him. "That field has to be somewhere."

So we went back to the beacon's position and I began an ever-increasing spiral around the supposed position of the beacon . . . in the fog . . . where I could see vertically only 150 to 200 feet.

Finally, we found the field exactly on the reciprocal—180° opposite—of the number we'd been given at the briefing!

The field was totally covered with Allied fighter planes—P-51s, P-38s, and P-37s, all grounded due to the fog—and no space to park a B-17. As I made a turn to line up for the runway I could see green flares signaling the okay for a landing.

Woody reduced his air speed to prepare for the landing when suddenly he saw another B-17 taxiing directly toward them in the center of the runway. Landing at that point would have meant two dead B-17 crews. Forced back into the air, Woody managed to lift his wing just enough to miss the wing of the oncoming aircraft by a few feet.

Flying at just 125 knots, it seemed impossible that he could gain altitude, let alone control the plane. *But after several minutes, the speed started to increase; I'd been traveling up a small hill. I soon got it up to 135 knots and started to climb, and after gaining about 500 feet, I went back to the beacon and then was able to go directly to the field. I held the plane at*

---

5 New airfields were established as the Allies advanced towards Germany. Woody noted that the line had moved forty miles across Belgium in the month between his first and second emergency landings.

about 150 feet to check for unknown traffic, made proper runway alignment and proceeded to make a landing. A third of the runway was already used up so I made a rudder walk-stall[6] *the last 150 feet of altitude and, in the last few feet, pushed the nose down to get just enough airspeed to make a decent flare.*[7] *I landed on the last third of the runway, smashing a searchlight that marked the far end of the runway and rolling off the end into thick mud. After we came to a full stop, the crew piled out. We had made it! And with just one injury...*

On landing, there were no fire trucks standing by. The fire crew had heard the number 2 engine misfiring as we went around and they knew we couldn't make it back, so they took off to look for us, assuming we would crash.

We were all dog-tired, but no one got a chance to relax. We each had an hour and a half of debriefing, then went to the mess hall to eat. By the time we got to the barracks, about 40 other Allied airmen, still grounded and waiting for the weather to improve, were hanging around waiting to ask me how I did it.

"How do you make a turn with just two engines on one side and get lined up without having your wing hit the ground and roll the airplane?" they wanted to know. They kept me up till after midnight asking all sorts of technical questions, trying to understand how we survived with such a damaged airplane.

Finally I told them, "That's it for the night, guys. I need some shut-eye." They said, "Man, what a guy," and they wrote a letter to our commanding officer giving me all sorts of kudos.

Earl Valentine's post-mission notes summarized the day—again in clipped and understated language: *Twelfth Mission: Hit tank factory at Plauen. Flak light and accurate. Got hit (flak) back of No. 2 engine ...Saw Painter's ship hit and blow up. Jets (total 15) hit again... They seemed to concentrate on our ship. Had five very heavy hits, two in right wing, one in left, and left horizontal stabilizer nearly shot away, each hole about three foot square. One 30mm exploded in radio room. Fell out of formation and*

---

6 Rudder walk-stall: rapidly and forcefully alternating full left and right rudder, causing the aircraft to slow down brusquely and quickly decrease altitude (the way a leaf oscillates as it drops from a tree, but much more rapidly).
7 Flare: Pulling up on the elevator to bring the nose of the aircraft up, increasing the pitch and thus controlling the fall and forward motion.

struggled on to Belgium base. Ship controlled by only two battered cables; jettisoned all equipment possible. Left ship #503 to be salvaged; flew back in C-47 and landed at Limey base. Hlavka [the gunner] *hit by small piece in leg. That mission is one none of us will ever forget, could be called Rough.*

Woody added that once again he and his crew were labeled Missing in Action for the several days that it took them to return to England, since nobody in their squadron saw them after they were hit by the Me 262 jets and they descended into the clouds. Being MIA was not all bad, however, as Earl Valentine's log records that he and his fellow crewmembers *stayed in Brussels one night, went swimming and had* [an] *enjoyable time.*

Following Woody's return to Thorpe Abbotts, his squadron took part in thirteen more bombing missions. Woody's fellow crews joked that if he was flying, everybody else was safe because all the action would be directed at him.

Woody by this time was flying as the squadron's deputy lead, meaning he occupied the center position in the formation, with a plane on each wing, three more above and below him, and three at the rear. (As Woody explained, new pilots were always assigned to the rear so their skills could be assessed before they were positioned with other planes. His own first flight from Thorpe Abbotts had been as "Tail-end Charlie.")

Woody added that the planes took off at 30-second intervals—which was the amount of time it took them, loaded with bombs, to get into the air. They would then meet up over the English Channel with squadrons from other bomb groups that were based at other nearby airfields. The 100th bomb group was identifiable by a big 'D' painted on the tails of the aircraft, and the planes in each group flew together. To help pilots get into formation in the pre-dawn dark, the lead pilot in each group would fire a color-coded triple flare from a vary-pistol while flying in a broad circle, so as to give the other planes time to catch up and get into position.

Between April 3 and April 8, 1945, Woody's squadron was sent out six days in a row. On April 7, their mission was to bomb the oil storage tanks at Buchen, near Hamburg. Again they were attacked by fighters, though not the lethal Me 262s. Earl Valentine reported: *Continuous attacks for about thirty minutes on our group. Saw two B-17s go down, one blew up real close to us. Prior to fighter attacks saw several chutes going down from the groups ahead of us. One Me 109 crashed into a B-17 and another one crashed into two of them… Weather was visual but missed target… No hits on* [our] *ship. Was a rough day.*

The next day, April 8, they went out again, this time to bomb the airfield at Munich. Valentine's log registered: *Longest straight haul in history. Flak was inaccurate. Weather was good and saw hits. Snow capped mountains* [the Bavarian Alps] *were very beautiful.*

By this time, the Allied forces had made rapid advances against the German armies and had crossed the Rhine into Germany itself. On April 20, 1945, Hitler's 56th birthday, the 350th Squadron, including the "Heaven Sent," completed its 25th and last bombing mission over railway marshaling yards six miles north of Berlin. Valentine wrote that on their return they went over Hanover, Brunswick, Essen, Dortmund and Dusseldorf, *all in ruins.*

The war still had several weeks to run, however, and Woody and his crew still had work to do. A pocket of Holland was still occupied by the Germans, and the greater Dutch population, having suffered through what was called *Hongerwinter* (Hunger Winter), was starving. The country's bridges and railroads had been destroyed by the retreating Nazis, canals were frozen over, and farmlands were flooded. Those people who were able to resorted to frying or boiling sugar beets and prized tulip bulbs for food.

Woody recounted accordingly: *As the war turned against the Germans, their surviving leaders realized they would need some goodwill for the Post-War, so they brokered a deal to have American planes drop food over Holland in return for an agreement not to land in territory still occupied.*

On May 1, the day after Hitler's suicide, Woody and his crew volunteered for a humanitarian mission to make food-drops over Holland. The bomb bays of the B-17s were modified with a thick plywood platform, hinged on the outside and hung on the inside by cables connecting to the bomb-release shackles. The platform was loaded with tons of K-rations and, upon reaching their destination, the B-17 crews discharged their cargo into fishing nets the Dutch had strung up between telephone poles placed along soccer fields. *They laid white sheets in the shape of crosses in front of the nets to provide a target for us. As with all the Lowlands, there was almost always fog. The fields had no instrument facilities for flying guidance, so we had to do all our navigation by dead reckoning . . . in fog, with no more than 200 feet vertical visibility.*[8] *On my first food drop, as we passed over Rotterdam, a man on a rooftop copied my tail numbers as a means to contact us. After the War, he wrote me a letter and gave it to the first Spitfire pilot who landed in Rotterdam. That pilot forwarded the letter to me.*

After the war in Europe finally came to an end, Woody flew both people and freight on various missions over Europe and North Africa. On one occasion, his group was assigned to pick up and fly home to Paris a group of French citizens who had been liberated from Nazi concentration camps. *I will never forget that day. When they boarded the plane they each carried a rusty 5-lb. coffee can. When I asked "Why?" the lead man looked at me as if to say, "How can you be so stupid? . . . That was our toilet." It* [was] *difficult to understand the deprivation these people endured . . .*

As we flew across the Rhine River toward Paris, I let them come to the cockpit to follow the terrain on the map. Without exception, they all shed tears as they realized they were at last free.

After the War, Woody returned to his studies at UCLA and earned his degree in scientific instrumentation and electrical chemistry. He hired me (Don) to work with him and we became long-time friends. One of things that struck me about him was that while some guys who fought in the war never forgave the Germans, Woody wasn't one of them. He said you had to treat combat as "a contest of war, not a person-to-person contest." At least, that's how he saw it. He added, however, that if he'd been on a beach front and somebody had been trying to stab him with a bayonet, then it might have got "real personal, real fast."

Early in 2013, Réanne and I told Woody's story to John Slagboom, the newly-elected Commodore of our local Yacht Club, a Dutchman who had been a teenager during WWII. John was eager to get in touch with Woody, because he realized that Woody's B-17 had probably been the plane that dropped tons of K-Rations over his town as he stood on the roof of one of the houses. John made contact with Woody by email and the two set a

---

8 Dead reckoning required keeping track of the speed and time and how long it was running on that course so they could calculate the distance from the last known position.

date to meet at the Blondfield's home in Apple Valley. Tragically, on April 18, 2013—three days before their meeting, and as this book was being completed—Woody died unexpectedly.

We include here John's letter to Woody, which was read at the memorial service.

April 18 2013

Good Morning Woody,
Today is the day we were going to meet each other, at 1000 hours. That was the plan. Well, Woody, the last time we met was in Holland on April 15, 1945. You were flying over our heads at treetop level in a B-17—the biggest airplane—with open doors and unloading, on the fly, tons of food only a starving boy can imagine. That was the best bombing we had ever seen.

Our part of Holland was still occupied and there was nothing to eat. (I ate my neighbors' cat, but don't tell anybody.) You saved many lives that day—that winter was known as Hunger Winter. We found out that you volunteered for that mission. THANKS, WOODY. That food drop made you my Hero forever.

Can I tell you how you changed my life, Woody? During the German occupation (my age 12 to 17), our first school was taken over by the German troops. The second school was too close to the Allied bombing raids and was shut down. All that was fine with me (I didn't like schooling anyway). Families were torn apart and each on his own. After the war, my passion was flying. (That's where you came in.)

I had no money, but I had a plan . . . Go to the USA. That was my plan. Sign up as a sailor in the Merchant Marine. And walk off the boat in America. Well, that boat went to South America instead, and I walked off in Buenos Aires, Argentina. But eleven years later, in 1958, I migrated to the USA. Woody, the story is more complex, but simply, you are my inspiration that helped make it happen.

So long, Woody. I will see you upstairs.
John Slagboom

Throughout his life, Woody set an example of strong ethical values. As a deputy squadron leader he served with distinction and is remembered not only for his skill in bringing his crew through the events described in this chapter, but also for volunteering for the humanitarian missions over Holland. He was proud of his crew and honored their trust and devotion in everything they did together and asked that we recognize those men whose names are cited below:

Elwood (Woody) Blondfield: Pilot
James L Dizmang: Co-pilot
Norman E. La Montagne (Monty): Navigator
Royal L. Brooks: Flight Engineer
Lawrence F. Hlavka: Radio Operator
Lloyd N. Wells: Ball Turret Gunner
Edward J. Markuten: Gunner
Clarence R. Sanders: Gunner
Earl H. Valentine: Tail Gunner

Woody Blondfield and his wife Bebe, 2011

Woody shows off one of the silk maps supplied with his 'escape kit.'

GLOSSARY

Abwehr: German military counter-intelligence.

Ausweis: German permit to enter forbidden coastal zone.

B-17 (Flying Fortress): American four-engine heavy bomber with crew of 10.

B-24 (Liberator): American four-engine heavy bomber with crew of 11.

Colis: Packages—the Shelburne Line's term for aviators transferred from Paris to Brittany.

Dulag: German transit camp.

Enigma: Highly secret German cryptographic machine.

ETO: European Theater of Operations.

FFL (*Forces Françaises Libres*): Free French Forces.

FFI (*Forces Françaises de l'Interieur*): French Forces of the Interior.

Flak: Anti-aircraft fire (from the German *Flag Abwehr Kanone*).

Gestapo: German Secret State Police (from *Geheime Staatspolizei*)

Halifax: Four-engine heavy bomber used by the RAF.

KIA: Killed in Action

Lancaster: Four-engine bomber carrying 7 men.

Lysander: Light single-engine airplane used for clandestine night landings.

Maquis: Loosely organized French Underground fighters who took to the "brush" or mountains (from Corsican word literally meaning "the brush").

Maquisard: Member of the *Maquis*.

Me 109 (Messerchmitt): German fighter aircraft.

Me 262 (Messerchmitt): German jet fighter aircraft

MGB: Motor Gun Boat.

MIA: Missing in Action.

MI-9: British Military Intelligence in charge of aviator escape and evasion.

Milice: Vichy French police (similar to Gestapo), greatly feared by the population.

Milicien: Officer of the *Milice*.

Oflag (*Offizierslager*): German Prisoner of War camp for officers.

Pick-Up: Operation to recover an individual after a clandestine landing.

POW: Prisoner of War.

RAF; RCAF: (British) Royal Air Force; Royal Canadian Air Force.

Room 900: Office within MI-9 designated to assist with evacuations from Belgium and France.

SAS: Special Air Service founded by the British in 1941 to train and arm local fighters. The SAS was sent to Brittany after D-Day to carry out Operation Lost for three weeks in June-July of 1944.

SOE: Special Operations Executive—British Intelligence Agency in charge of subversive operations.

SS (*Shutzstaffel*): Feared German paramilitary defense organization.

Stalag: POW camp for non-commissioned military.

STO (*Service du Travail Obligatoire*): Compulsory labor service for young French men born between 1920-22 to supply workers for German factories. The STO was set up in 1943 to conscript 500,000 men to work in Germany.

USAAF: United States Army Air Force.

WASPs: Women Airforce Service Pilots.

Bibliography

Air Forces Escape & Evasion Society. Paducah, KY: Turner Publishing Co., 1992.

Aron, Robert. *Histoire de la Libération de la France.* Paris: Librairie Arthème Fayard, 1959.

Aubrac, Lucie. *Ils Partiront dans l'Ivresse,* Editions du Seuil, 1984. (Good resource for Resistance movement in general; particularly for the movements in Southern France.)

Aubrac, Lucie. *Outwitting the Gestapo.* Lincoln: University of Nebraska Press, 1993. English translation varies somewhat from the original French edition.

Beevor, Antony. *D-Day: the Battle for Normandy.* New York: Viking, 2009.

Bloch, Marc. *Strange Defeat; A Statement of Evidence Written in 1940.* New York: W.W. Norton, 1968; reissued 1999.

Bodson, Herman. *Downed Allied Airmen and Evasion of Capture: The Role of Local and Resistance Networks in World War II.* Jefferson, NC: McFarland & Company, Inc., 2005.

Boeselager, Philipp Freiherr von. *Valkyrie: The Story of the Plot to Kill Hitler, by its Last Member.* New York: Vintage Books, 2010.

Bowman, Martin W. *Home by Christmas? The Story of US Airmen at War.* Wellingborough, England: Patrick Stephens, 1987.

Brokaw, Tom. *The Greatest Generation.* New York: Random House, 1998.

Caine, Philip D. *Aircraft Down! Evading Capture in WWII Europe.* Washington D.C.: Potomac Books, Inc., 1997.

Camby, Philippe. *La Libération de la Bretagne.* Rennes: Ouest France, 1980.

Churchill, Winston S. *Triumph and Tragedy,* Vol. 6 of *The Second World War.* Cambridge, MA: Houghton Mifflin, 1953.

Churchill, Winston S. (grandson), ed. *Never Give In! The Best of Winston Churchill's Speeches.* New York: Hyperion, 2003.

Dear, Ian and Kemp, Peter. *A-Z of Sailing Terms.* Oxford: Oxford University Press, 1997.

Dolitsky, Alexander B., ed. *Allies in Wartime: The Alaska-Siberia Airway During World War II.* Juneau: Alaska-Siberia Research Center, 2007.

Doyle, Robert C. *A Prisoner's Duty: Great Escapes in U.S. Military History.* New York: Bantam Books, 1997.

Dumais, Lucien A. *Un Canadien Français Face à la Gestapo.* Montreal: Editions du Jour, 1969.

Dumais, Lucien A. *The Man Who Went Back.* London: Futura Publications Limited, 1974.

Fest, Joachim. *Les derniers jours de Hitler.* Tours: Editions Perrin, 2002.

Fichou, Jean-Christophe. *Les Pêcheurs Bretons Durant la Seconde Guerre Mondiale.* Rennes: Presses Universitaires de Rennes, 2009.

Foot, M.R.D. and J.M. Langley. *MI 9.* London: The Bodley Head Ltd., 1979.

Fowler, Will. *Special Forces Guide to Escape and Evasion.* New York: St. Martin's Press, 2005.

Garnier, Jean-Pierre (transl.). Assorted pamphlets published by ARSA (Association Rhodanienne pour le Souvenir Aérien). Rhône Valley, France.

Gaspin, Jordan. *De la "Drôle de guerre" à la victoire (1939-1945).* Rennes: Editions Ouest-France, 2010.

Glass, Charles. *Americans in Paris: Life & Death Under Nazi Occupation.* New York: Penguin Books, 2009.

Gould, John Van Wyck. *The Last Dog in France: A Tale of the French Resistance and Their Escape Line in WWII.* Bloomington, Indiana: AuthorHouse, 2006.

Guillet, Laurent. *Nous étions ennemis!* Imprimerie de Guingamp: Privately published, 2007.

Halbrook, Stephen P. *The Swiss and the Nazis.* Philadelphia: Casemate, 2010.

Hochart, Jacques & Berrier, Marie. *World War II Allied Airmen Who Fell from the Sky Over Dunkirk and the Surrounding Area.* Marck, France: Association Souvenirs de Pierres, Revised Ed., 2010.

Huguen, Roger. *La Bretagne dans la bataille de l'Atlantique.* Spézet: Coop Breizh, 2003.

Huguen, Roger. *Par les Nuits les Plus Longues: Réseau d'évasion d'aviateurs en Bretagne* 1940-1944. Spézet: Coop Breizh, 1993; 10th Edition, 2003.

Jackson, Julian. France: *The Dark Years 1940-1944*. Oxford: Oxford University Press, 2001.

Janes, Peter Scott. *Conscript Heroes*. Great Britain: Paul Mould Publishers. 2004.

Jégouzo, Yves. *Madeleine dite Betty*: Déportée résistante à Auschwitz-Birkenau. Paris: L'Harmattan, 2011.

Jourdan-Joubert, Louis; Julien Helfgott, Pierre Golliet. *Glières: Premiere bataille de la Résistance*. Annecy: L'Association des Rescapés des Glières, 1946.

Jouvent, Georges. *Enfant du Dauphiné: Années Vingt – Années Quarantes*. Fontaine: Editions ThoT, 2005.

Kladstrup, Don & Petie. *Wine & War: The French, the Nazis & the Battle for France's Greatest Treasure*. New York: Broadway Books, 2001.

Lavender, Emerson and Sheffe, Norman. *The Evaders. True Stories of Downed Canadian Airmen and Their Helpers in World War II*. Toronto: McGraw Hill-Ryerson, 1992.

Le Nédélec, Alain. *Les Nuits de la Liberté, Les évasions par Plouha*. Saint-Brieuc: Presses Bretonnes, 1993.

Le Trividic, Dominique-Martin. *Une Héroine de la Résistance: Marie-Thérèse Le Calvez du réseau Shelburn*. Rennes: Editions Ouest-France, 2002.

Ledwidge, Bernard. *De Gaulle*. New York: St. Martin's Press, 1982.

Lenburg, John L. *Kriegsgefangenen #6410: Prisoner of War*. San Jose, CA: Writers Club Press, 2002.

Liddell-Hart, B.H., ed. *The Rommel Papers*. New York: De Capo Press, 1953.

Lieb, Peter. *Vercors 1944: Resistance in the French Alps*. Oxford: Osprey Publishing, 2012.

Litoff, Judy Barrett, ed. *An American Heroine in the French Resistance: The Diary and Memoir of Virginia d'Albert-Lake*. New York: Fordham University Press, 2006.

McIntosh, Elizabeth P. *Sisterhood of Spies: Women of the OSS*. Annapolis, MD: Naval Institute Press, 1998.

McNab, Chris. *Escape and Evasion.* Broomall, PA: Mason Crest Publishers, 2003.

McNab, Chris. *Surviving Captivity with the U.S. Air Force.* Broomall, PA: Mason Crest Publishers, 2003.

Maitland, Leslie. *Crossing the Borders of Time: A True Story of War, Exile, and Love Reclaimed.* New York: Other Press, 2012.

Manchester, William. *The Last Lion: Winston Spencer Churchill.* New York: Dell Publishing, 1983.

Metcalf, Jonathan, ed. *La Seconde Guerre Mondiale: de la Montée de Nazisme à la Victoire des Alliés.* Paris: 2010. Translated into French by Cédric Perdereau. (Originally published by Dorling Kindersley in 2009 under the title World War II)

Michel, Florence. *Michel Sardou.* Paris: Editions Seghers, 1985.

Monnier, Jean-Jacques. *Résistance et Conscience Bretonne, 1940-1945.* Fouesnant: Yoran Embanner, 2007.

Montaz, Pierre. *Onze Américains Tombés du Ciel.* Bourg d'Oisans: Artès, 1994; 2010.

Montaz, Pierre. *Les Pionniers du Téléski.* Meylan: Pierre Montaz, 2006.

Moorehead, Caroline. *A Train in Winter.* New York: Harper Collins, 2011.

Morris, Rob. *Untold Valor: Forgotten Stories of American Bomber Crews Over Europe in World War II.* Washington D.C.: Potomac Books, Inc., 2006.

Moser, Joseph F. *A Fighter Pilot in Buchenwald.* Bellingham, WA: Edens Veil Media, 2009.

Neave, Airey. *Escape Room.* New York: Tower Publications, 1969.

Neave, Airey. *Saturday at M.I.9.* London: Hodder and Stoughton, 1969.

Ottis, Sherri Greene. *Silent Heroes: Downed Airmen and the French Underground.* Lexington: University Press of Kentucky, 2001.

Patton, Ralph K. *Flying on a Wing and a Prayer: How the Army Air Corps Trained Me and the French Resistance Saved Me.* Privately Published: 2011

Paxton, Robert O. *Vichy France, Old Guard and New Order, 1940-1944.* New York: Columbia University Press, 1972, 2001.

Peyrefitte, Alain et al. *De Gaulle 1940-1958.* Saint-Amand: Editions Tallandier, 1998.

Pitchfork, Graham. *Shot Down and on the Run: The RCAF and Commonwealth Aircrews Who Got Home from Behind Enemy Lines, 1940-1945.* Toronto: The Dundurn Group, 2003.

Quellien, Jean. *La Résistance.* Cully, France: OREP Editions, 2007.

Quétel, Claude. *La Seconde Guerre Mondiale.* Caen: Editions Mémorial de Caen, 2003.

Quereillahc, Jean-Louis. *Le STO Pendant la Seconde Guerre Mondiale.* Paris: De Borée, 2010.

Rémy. *Autour de la Plage Bonaparte.* Paris: Librairie Académique Perrin, 1969.

Richards, Brooks. *Secret Flotillas, Vol. I. Clandestine Sea Operations to Brittany 1940-1944.* London: Frank Cass Publishers, 2004.

Roberts, Andrew. *The Storm of War: A New History of the Second World War.* New York: HarperCollins, 2011.

Rondel, Eric. *Les Américains en Bretagne, 1944-1945.* Sables-d'Or-les-Pins: Editions Astoure, 2008.

Rondel, Eric. *Collaboration et épuration en Bretagne.* Sables-d'Or-les-Pins: Editions Astoure, 2009.

Rondel, Eric. *En Attendant le Débarquement du 15 août 1943 au 6 juin 1944.* Sables-d'Or-les-Pins: Editions Astoure, 2011.

Saigal, Monique. *Héroïnes françaises, 1940-1945, Courage, force et ingéniosité.* Monaco: Editions du Rocher, 2008.

Shirer, William L. *The Collapse of the Third Republic.* New York: Simon and Schuster, 1969.

Toland, John. *Adolf Hitler.* New York: Ballantine Books, 1976.

Tursi, John and Thelma Palmer. *Long Journey to the Rose Garden.* Anacortes, WA: Fidalgo Bay Publishing, 1989.

Verity, Hugh. *We Landed by Moonlight. The Secret RAF Landing in France 1940-1944.* Manchester, England: Crecy Publishing, Revised Ed. 2000.

Vinen, Richard. *The Unfree French: Life under the Occupation.* New Haven: Yale University Press, 2006.

Weitz, Margaret Collins. *Sisters in the Resistance: How Women Fought to Free France, 1940-1945.* New York: John Wiley & Sons, 1995.

Wieviorka, Olivier. *Histoire du Débarquement en Normandie.* Paris: Editions du Seuil, 2007.

BIBLIOGRAPHY

INTERVIEWS & CORRESPONDENCE

Blakely, C.W. Personal papers, correspondence and photos, 2011-2014.

Blondfield, Elwood. Recorded interviews by RHD and DCD, correspondence and telephone conversations. Apple Valley, California. 2009-2013.

Carter, Gordon. Recorded interviews by RHD and DCD, Quimper, France; correspondence, photos; papers, 2010, 2011.

Giquel, Marie (Mimi). Interview, 2009.

Garnier, Jean-Pierre. Correspondence.

Janin, Robert. Interviews 2007-2012.

Jouvent, Marie-Thérèse Le Meur. Interviews 2007-2010.

Le Saux-Pierre, Marguérite (Guiguite). Interviews; telephone; correspondence 2009-2013.

Mainguy, Joseph. *Le Réseau d'Evasion Shelburn* [sic] *Pat O'Leary à l'Anse Cochat en Plouha. "Plage Bonaparte."* Handwritten manuscript courtesy of Beverly Patton Wand.

Montaz, Pierre. Interviews & Correspondence 2012-2014.

Ropers, Anne. Interviews 2009-2013.

Scovill, Nancy Costello. Correspondence, telephone, photographs. 2011-2014

Sorgenfrei, Kennon. Interview 2012; telephone; papers; photos 2012-2014

Tréhiou, Jean. Interviews 2009-2010.

Valentine, Earl. Correspondence, telephone, photos, 2011-2014.

Wand, Beverly Patton. Personal papers of Ralph Patton, maps, photos, correspondence and telephone, 2011-2012.

Warren, Geoff. Interview, correspondence, papers and telephone, 2011.

Photo Credits

All photographs supplied by author, except where otherwise credited.

Chapter 2

RAF Lysander over France, WWII. (Photo credit: Ken Mist)

Chapter 4

Motor Gun Boat 503 underway. (Photo credit: Air Forces Escape & Evasion Society.)

Maps in this chapter are adapted from hand-drawn originals by Joseph Mainguy.

Chapter 5

An example of a *gazogène*-fueled vehicle, France, WWII. (Photo credit: fr.wikipedia.org)

Chapter 6

Whiz wheel. (Photo courtesy of Nancy Costello Scovill.)

Robert Costello's fake French ID card (Photo courtesy of Nancy Costello Scovill.)

Chapter 9

Gordon Carter in his RAF uniform. (Photo courtesy of Gordon Carter.)

Halifax, WWII. (Photo credit: en.wikipedia.org)

Carter's Halifax bomber, on the ground in France. (Photo courtesy of Gordon Carter.)

Gordon and Janine after the war. (Photo courtesy of Gordon Carter.)

Gordon Carter speaking at a Resistance commemoration, c. 2000. (Photo courtesy of Gordon Carter.)

Chapter 10

Chick Blakley in uniform. (Photo courtesy of Chick Blakley.)

The crew of the 'Ram It-Dam It.' (Photo courtesy of Chick Blakley.)

BIBLIOGRAPHY

Chapter 11

Robert Janin at 16-17. (Photo courtesy of Robert Janin.)

Robert in French army uniform, age 18. (Photo courtesy of Robert Janin.)

Chapter 12

The Le Meur house & café. (Photo courtesy of Pascale Jouvent Chaumont.)

The Le Meur-Jouvent family, 1956. (Photo courtesy of Pascale Jouvent Chaumont.)

Geo and Marité, 1956. (Photo courtesy of Pascale Jouvent Chaumont.)

Photos on pages 146 and 150 purchased from Les Archives de Calvados.

Chapter 13

B-24 pilot Ken Sorgenfrei with his crew. (Photo courtesy of Ken Sorgenfrei.)

Members of Ken Sorgenfrei's crew. (Photo courtesy of Ken Sorgenfrei.)

Makeshift *Maquis* 'hospital'. (Photo courtesy of Pierre Montaz.)

Maps in this chapter are courtesy of Pierre Montaz.

Chapter 14

B-17s in action, WWII. (Photo courtesy of Woody Blondfield.)

Woody and crew. (Photo courtesy of Woody Blondfield.)

The 'Heaven Sent.' (Photo courtesy of Woody Blondfield.)

Front cover photograph by Réanne Douglass. The B-17, *Liberty Belle* (J 297848)—one of about a dozen restored WWII aircraft in the U.S.— was a "flying museum." In May 2011 during one of her tours, Don and I were privileged to have a flight around Puget Sound from Boeing Field. On June 13, 2011, during a tour a few weeks after this photo was taken, one of her engines caught fire and she made a forced landing in a cornfield in Oswego, Illinois. The plane burned and blew up before fire fighters could reach her. Fortunately, no lives were lost.

ABOUT THE AUTHOR

Réanne Hemingway-Douglass grew up in the Great Lakes region and Washington D.C. She attended Pomona College, Claremont Graduate University in Southern California, and the Université de Grenoble, France. After teaching French for twenty years, she joined her husband, Don Douglass, in their manufacturing and backpacking business. In the 1970s she and Don were the first American couple to attempt a circumnavigation of the Southern Hemisphere by sailboat. Her book *Cape Horn: One Man's Dream, One Woman's Nightmare* tells the story of their pitchpoling near Cape Horn. In her fifties, Réanne and a friend were the first women to bicycle across Tierra del Fuego. Réanne's articles on bicycling, cruising and women's issues have appeared in numerous outdoor magazines. In addition to annual visits to her French "families," Réanne and Don have bicycled, hiked and boated extensively in what she considers to be her "second country." She and Don are the authors of a series of six detailed nautical guidebooks and maps from Baja Mexico to Prince William Sound, Alaska and, from 1986-2004, they were the publishers/owners of Fine Edge Productions. The Douglasses currently live on Fidalgo Island in Washington State and have recently established a new publishing imprint, Cave Art Press, with more projects underway.

Réanne and Don Douglass in the French Alps.

Masterfully painting details of suspense and intrigue, Hemingway-Douglass tells a great story of unsung heroes in the French Underground who risked everything to save downed Allied airmen. Blending recorded history with first person accounts, this is a gripping narrative that even prolific war storywriters like W.E.B. Griffin and Alistair MacLean would have to admire.
—John La Raia, Lt. Col. USAF (Ret.)